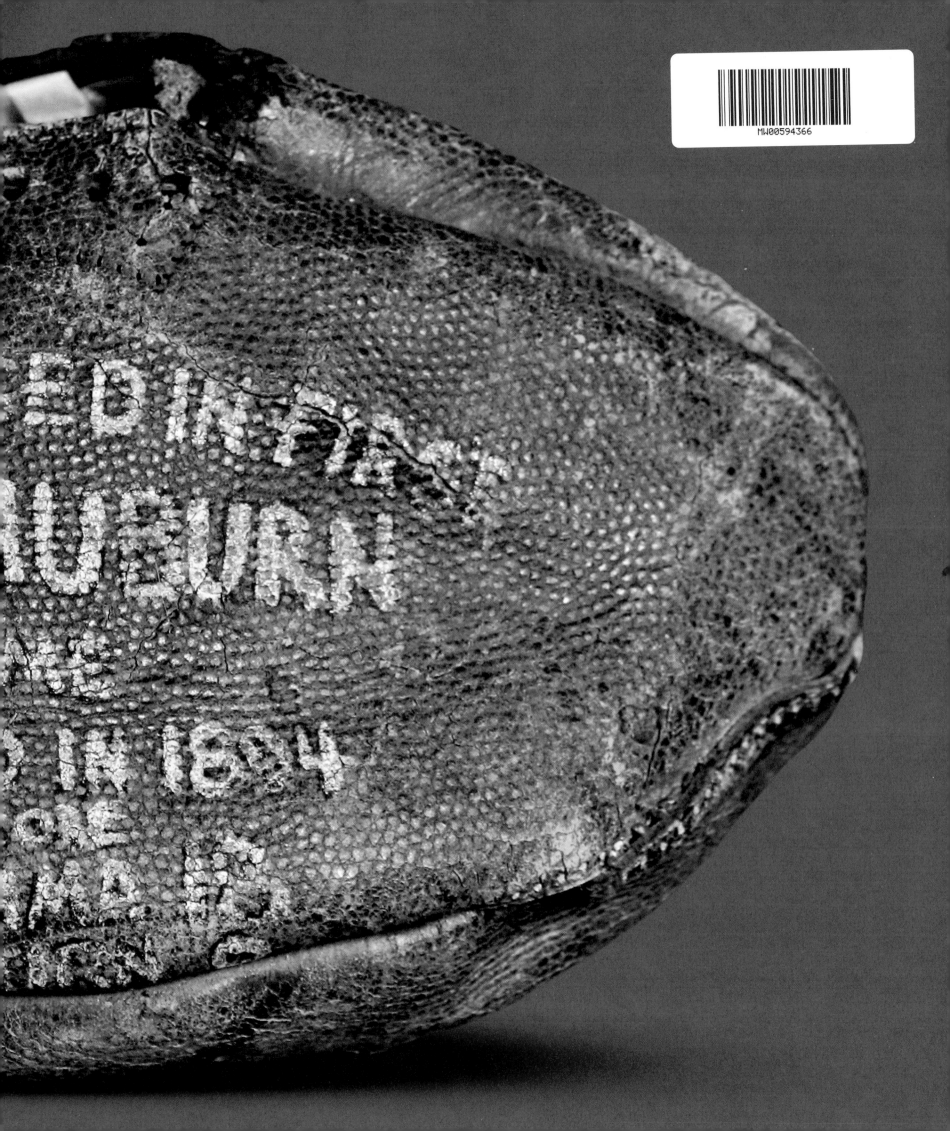

Sports Illustrated

ALABAMA FOOTBALL

Among those who have worn number 12: Bear Bryant, Joe Namath, Kenny Stabler and Greg McElroy.

2010
HALLELUJAH MOMENT
After his late touchdown put the BCS title game
out of reach, Mark Ingram let his exultation show.
Photograph by ROBERT BECK

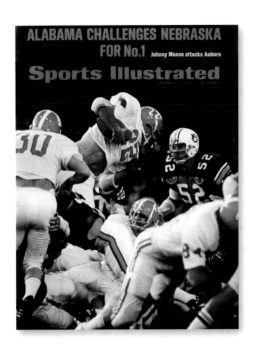

ALABAMA CHALLENGES NEBRASKA
FOR No.1 Johnny Musso attacks Auburn

Sports Illustrated

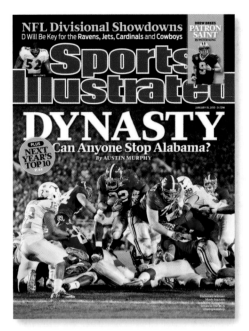

NFL Divisional Showdowns
D Will Be Key for the Ravens, Jets, Cardinals and Cowboys

DREW BREES
PATRON
SAINT
BY PETER KING

Sports Illustrated

DYNASTY
Can Anyone Stop Alabama?

PLUS
NEXT
YEAR'S
TOP 10

By AUSTIN MURPHY

Sports Illustrated

ALABAMA IS THE BEST—FOR NOW

1

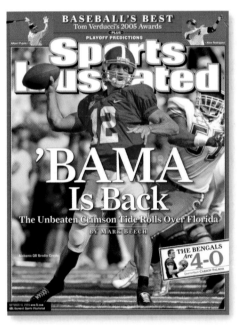

BASEBALL'S BEST
Tom Verducci's 2005 Awards
PLUS
PLAYOFF PREDICTIONS

Sports Illustrated

'BAMA
Is Back
The Unbeaten Crimson Tide Rolls Over Florida
BY MARK BEECH

THE BENGALS
Are
4-0

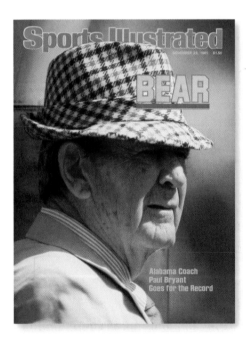

Sports Illustrated

BEAR

Alabama Coach
Paul Bryant
Goes for the Record

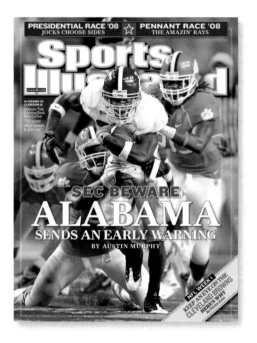

PRESIDENTIAL RACE '08
JOCKS CHOOSE SIDES
PENNANT RACE '08
THE AMAZIN' RAYS

Sports Illustrated

SEC BEWARE
ALABAMA
SENDS AN EARLY WARNING
BY AUSTIN MURPHY

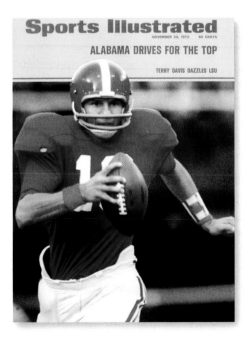

Sports Illustrated
NOVEMBER 20, 1972   65 CENTS

ALABAMA DRIVES FOR THE TOP

TERRY DAVIS DAZZLES LSU

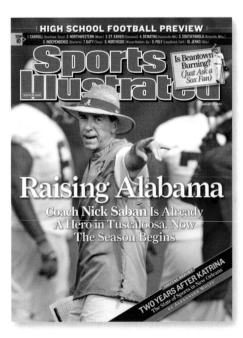

HIGH SCHOOL FOOTBALL PREVIEW

Sports Illustrated

Is Beantown
Burning?
(Just Ask a
Sox Fan)

Raising Alabama
Coach Nick Saban Is Already
A Hero in Tuscaloosa. Now
The Season Begins

TWO YEARS AFTER KATRINA
The State of Sports in New Orleans

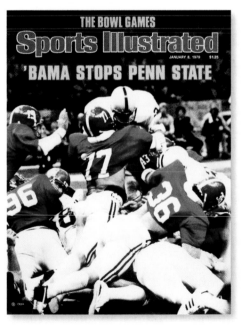

THE BOWL GAMES

Sports Illustrated
JANUARY 8, 1979 $1.25

'BAMA STOPS PENN STATE

![Sports Illustrated]

Contents

The 1931 Alabama helmet

Editor BILL SYKEN
Designer STEVEN HOFFMAN
Associate Designers JOSH DENKIN,
STEPHEN SKALOCKY
Photo Editor DON DELLIQUANTI
Copy Editor KEVIN KERR
Reporter ELIZABETH McGARR

1892
FIRST UNIT
Alabama's inaugural football team; founder William Little has the ball in hand.
Photograph by PAUL W. BRYANT MUSEUM/ UNIVERSITY OF ALABAMA

1973
GOOD CHEER
A young woman gets up in arms
during a 'Bama win over LSU.
Photograph by NEIL LEIFER

2006
THE HAT
This piece of Bearwear was shot at
the museum that, um, bears Bryant's name.
Photograph by BILL FRAKES

1962
QUARTERBACK COOL
Joe Namath as a sophomore,
when he was just getting started.
Photograph by NEIL LEIFER

2009
PERFECT BEGINNING
After an undefeated first year under center,
Greg McElroy's future was looking up.
Photographs by ROGELIO V. SOLIS/AP

1961

CHECK THE SCOREBOARD
This edition of the Iron Bowl was clearly
a happy one—for 'Bama fans, anyway.
Photograph by MARVIN E. NEWMAN

1974
OVERMATCHED
Few defenders stood a chance at getting
between Ozzie Newsome and a reception.
Photograph by PAUL W. BRYANT MUSEUM/
UNIVERSITY OF ALABAMA

2009
TOUCHDOWN TIME
This Colin Peek catch helped ensure the Tide's
win over Florida in the SEC title game.
Photograph by BILL FRAKES

1965
HORNS APLENTY
The Million Dollar Band is a
Tuscaloosa tradition all its own.
Photograph by JAY LEVITON/ATLANTA

1962

THE WATCHMEN

A panoramic view of the clean-cut guys on
the bench during a game at Tennessee.

Photograph by NEIL LEIFER

INTRODUCTION

CRIMSON PRIDE

BY ELI GOLD

IF THERE'S ONE THING I'VE LOVED THE MOST ABOUT BEING THE VOICE OF THE CRIMSON TIDE FOR TWENTY-TWO YEARS, IT'S THE FACT THAT FOR ALABAMA FOOTBALL FANS, THE SEASON NEVER REALLY ENDS. IN ALABAMA, PEOPLE TALK ABOUT FOOTBALL—COLLEGE FOOTBALL—ALL YEAR LONG. THEY LIVE IT AND BREATHE IT. THIS HAS BEEN TRUE FOR AS LONG AS THERE HAS BEEN A CRIMSON TIDE. AND IT GOES WAY BACK.

JUST BURSTING Fireworks were aflare as Nick Saban led his charges onto the field at the BCS championship game in Pasadena.

From the days of coach Wallace Wade's championships and Rose Bowl trips in the 1920s to coach Frank Thomas's championship run that stretched into the mid-1940s, 'Bama fans had plenty to talk about. Then, in the late '50s, a former Alabama player named Paul W. (Bear) Bryant returned to Tuscaloosa and gave fans not only something to talk, cheer and brag about for 20-plus years, but he also defined what it meant to be a winner and elevated the pride of the entire state along the way.

In the post-Bryant era, fans thrilled when coach Gene Stallings led an underdog team to the national championship in 1992, then never wavered when their patience was stretched to its limits during subsequent years of rebuilding. Support of their beloved Crimson Tide was, short of their own families, what they lived for.

When backing up my boast that the Alabama faithful are the best in the nation, I always used to say, "What other college team in the country gets 40,000 fans at their spring practice game?"

Then in 2007, Nick Saban took over and I had to amend that number. Make that 92,000 fans at the A-Day Game!

The fans have always been steadfast. But after coach Saban's arrival, we were newly plied with hopes and dreams being spun by a man whose résumé was replete with championships—a Big Ten title as a Michigan State assistant, a Mid-American Con-ference co-championship at Toledo and, of course, two SEC titles and a national championship at LSU.

We watched as Saban recruited some of the most talented players Alabama had seen in decades. (Some coaches recruit because they have to. Saban recruits because he loves to.) As much as he's known for his ability as an X's-and-O's coach, Saban showed himself to be a psychologist and a master motivator.

Then, after only his third season at the helm, 'Bama fans were rewarded with college football's most coveted prize when, on Jan. 7, 2010, Alabama bested Texas 37–21 in the BCS title game to win its 13th national championship.

How did this happen? There were many reasons for the Crimson Tide's flawless 2009 season. Great leadership from a coaching staff that was unmatched anywhere in the land. Outstanding players with skill, dedication and an eye on the job at hand. And most of all, desire.

From linebacker Rolando McClain, a surefire NFL first-round draft choice; to Alabama's first-ever Heisman Trophy winner, running back Mark Ingram; to the magnificent quarterback and game manager, Greg McElroy; every player on this team shared the common goal of winning a national title.

The players set this goal the minute they walked off the carpet at the Georgia Dome last year after losing to Florida in the SEC Championship game. They set the goal before they were back

GOOD TIDINGS Saban's first spring game attracted 92,000 fans who surely sensed that a return to glory was close at hand.

in the locker room. They said, "This ain't gonna happen again!"

So, from that moment on, through every push-up, every sit-up, every two-a-day workout, the Crimson Tide had an end in mind: getting to the SEC Championship to beat Florida and getting to the BCS championship game at the Rose Bowl Stadium to win the national title. If a player became tired during a workout and thought, I just can't do this anymore, he'd imagine another player on another team somewhere doing just a little bit more and he'd keep going. Every bead of sweat, every fraction of a second shaved off a sprint, meant the Tide was one step closer to its goal.

This was a team obsessed, and it showed on every game day. During the nail-biter against Tennessee, Terrence Cody's blocked field goal—his second of the day—on the last play preserved the undefeated season and moved Alabama closer to its goal. Against LSU, McElroy hooked up with Julio Jones on a 73-yard pass to salt away another crucial victory. Against Auburn, a late-game, field-long drive kept Alabama's rivals from spoiling a perfect season. And the SEC Championship? The emotional rematch against Florida, which Alabama dominated, turned out to be the Tide's ticket to Pasadena.

If you're a sports fan, watching a game at the Rose Bowl should be high on your bucket list. Ringed by the majestic San Gabriel Mountains, the place is vast, with more than

90,000 seats, and it's thrilling to see the expectant crowd in and around the stadium. It was exhilarating on game day for the Alabama players to walk in and see the crimson-wearing fans ringing the player's entrance to the stadium, thousands of them cheering wildly, as they do at every game, home and away. But it was especially uplifting to see so many of them out in California, when the national title was at stake.

I had broadcast from the Rose Bowl before, but never for a team playing for the national championship. The feeling is one that I'll never forget. Although most pundits had picked Alabama to win, those who watched closely knew that the outcome was far from certain: The Tide had lived and died by the run all season and they were facing the No. 1 rushing defense in America. But once again, this team found a way to win.

This book is the story of this special team and a special program. As I said to sign off our broadcast from Pasadena, "Alabama has just won its 13th national championship and the roses at this grand old stadium are once again crimson. . . ."

You, the fans, are a huge part of this championship and this story. You made it happen. Enjoy the book while reliving the pride. Roll Tide!

Eli Gold has been the radio play-by-play broadcaster for Crimson Tide football since 1988.

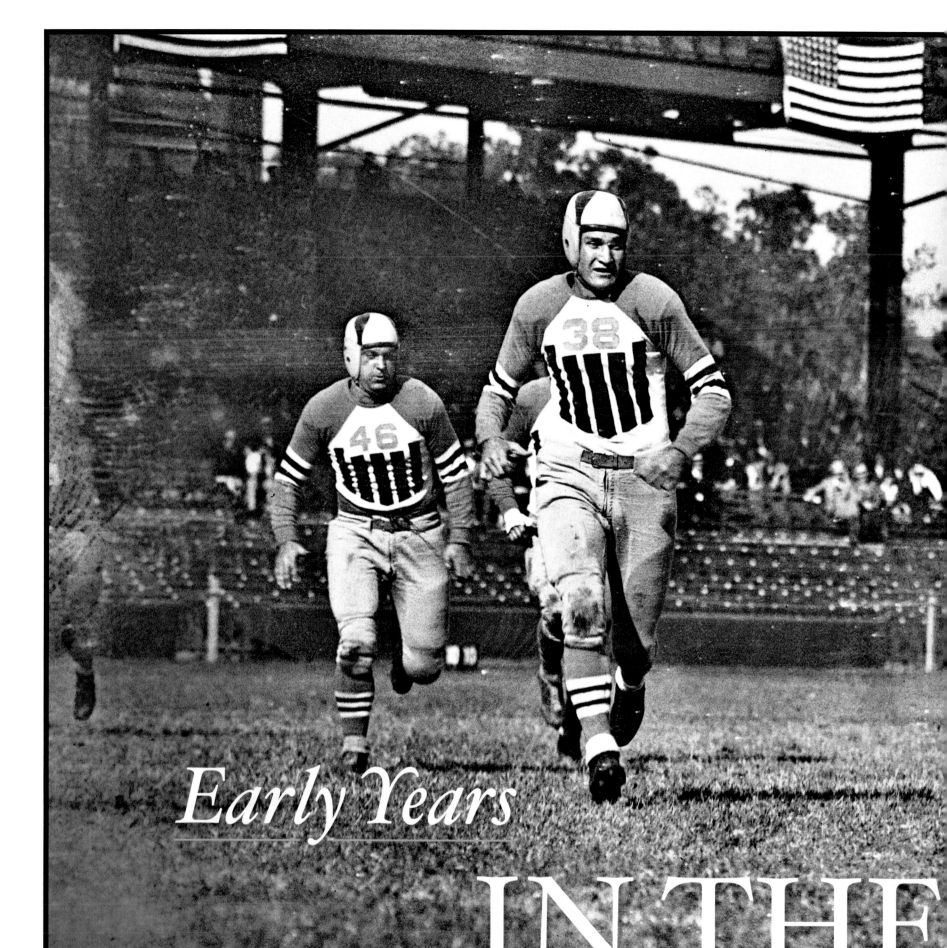

Early Years

IN THE

1932 | THE '30s were a good decade (two national titles) for the Tide; here John Cain (14) carries against George Washington University.

BEGINNING

BY FRANZ LIDZ · PHOTOGRAPH BY BETTMANN/CORBIS

Yes, Alabama did have a football program before Bear Bryant took over—in fact, a very good one. This story recounts the early heroes, nickname misfires (Crimson White?) and tells the surprising truth about where the university got the idea for starting a team. —*from* SI, AUGUST 30, 2006

L IKE A FOOTBALL FIELD AND A college football game, the history of the University of Alabama's football team is divided in half. *Anno Ursi* (Latin: "In the Year of the Bear"), abbreviated as AU or A.U., defines an epoch based on 1958, the year Paul Bryant was hired as coach. Similarly, Before Bear (from the Old English *bera*), abbreviated as BB or B.B., is used to denote years before the start of this era. In B.B. times the sacred saga of the Crimson Tide—not to be confused with the Red Sea—took on an almost Biblical dimension.

GENESIS

In the beginning, there was no team.

Though the university was founded in 1831, it wasn't until 1892 that a Yankee preppy named William Little brought the game to Tuscaloosa. The stocky, sturdy Livingston, Alabama-born lad had learned to play at Phillips Exeter Academy in New Hampshire, where he was being groomed for Yale. But the death of a brother forced Little to return home, where he enrolled at the university.

Bearing religious artifacts from the north—uniform, shoes and hallowed pigskin, Little organized a team and became Alabama's first gridiron evangelist. "Football is the game of the future in college life," he sermonized. "Players will be forced to live a most ascetic life, on a diet of rare beef and pork, to say nothing of rice pudding for dessert, for additional courage and fortitude, to stand the bumps and injuries."

Little was elected captain, and for a coach the university's newly formed Athletic Association hired an Ivy League dandy—derby-hatted, cane-brandishing Eugene Beauharnais Beaumont Jr., whose strongest credential was a membership on the "tug-of-war committee" at the University of Pennsylvania.

ALA-6 AUBURN-6

"A" GAME The guys ride high after tying Auburn in 1907.

On Nov. 11, 1892, the Cadets, as they called themselves, played a practice game that is now listed as their first official contest. They scrimmaged at a baseball park in Birmingham against a local high school pickup team. Dressed in white uniforms with red stockings and a large red UA stitched on their sweaters (but no helmets or shoulder pads), they romped 56–0, scoring 28 points in each half.

The big plays—including a 30-yard dash by Big Little, as 'Bama's 5' 11" captain was oxymoronically called—were run behind the Flying Wedge, a brutally effective formation introduced by Harvard earlier that year in a game against Yale. Over the next two decades so many crippling injuries and deaths (19 in 1904 alone!) in college ball were attributed to various wedges that by '05, at the behest of President Theodore Roosevelt, the configuration was outlawed.

Alabama faced its first legitimate opponent, the Birmingham Athletic Club, on Nov. 12. The Cadets—also known as the Varsity, the Capstones and the Crimson White—jumped out to a 4–0 lead on a Little touchdown. (Back then TDs counted four points.) But in the waning minutes, Birmingham's J.P. Ross, who had played rugby in Ireland, drop-kicked the ball 65 yards through the uprights. The astounding boot accounted for all of B.A.C.'s scoring (field goals were then worth five points) in the 5–4 victory. It would be the last time 'Bama lost by a single point until a 21–20 defeat at the hands of Tulane in 1947.

LAMENTATIONS

Alabama's final game that season was against Auburn at Lakefield Park in Birmingham. A crowd of 5,000 paid 25 cents admission to watch, and special trains arrived from Selma, Anniston and Montgomery. Cadets fans decked out the Caldwell Hotel with red and white banners.

Besides Big Little, the roster included Bibb Graves, who would later serve two terms as governor of the state, and William Bankhead, a future speaker of the U.S. House of Representatives and father of the actress Tallulah Bankhead. Auburn was loaded with frat boys—three from Sigma Nu, three Kappa Alphas, two Phi Delta Thetas and one Kappa Sigma. This Greek chorus was cheered on with rousing choruses of:

FOUNDING FATHER Little introduced football to the Tuscaloosa campus after learning to play at a Yankee prep school.

Preck-a-ge-gex! Preck-a-ge-gex!
Who-wah! Who-wah!
Hallaballoo!
Auburn!

The Alabama faithful countered with:

Hullabaloo, hooray, hooray
Hullabaloo, hooray, hooray
Hooray, hooray
Varsity, varsity
U of A.

In the end Hallaballoo trumped Hullabaloo, as Auburn beat Alabama 32–22, the most points 'Bama would score in a losing cause for 52 years. The excitement was summed up in a front-page story in *The Birmingham News*. "As the game ended, a series of cheers rent the air; the sun went down, blotting out the day of the greatest football game that was ever played in the state of Alabama."

Considering both colleges had been playing for less than two years, that wasn't saying a whole lot.

EXODUS

Over their first decade the Cadets had nearly as many coaches as victories. Beaumont finished at one and out. He was the first, but not the last, Alabama coach to be fired after losing to Auburn. In 1893 *The Corolla*, the official college yearbook, brusquely observed, "We were unfortunate in securing a coach. After keeping him for a short time, we found that his knowledge of the game was very limited. We therefore got rid of him."

Beaumont begat Eli Abbott, a tackle and fullback on the '92–94 teams (and coach of the '93–95 teams). A ringer from Penn who had been lured away from his job as a foreman on Warrior River Lock 17, Abbott was not only 'Bama's second coach but also, in 1902, briefly its eighth. Alas, he had better luck on the field (he scored four times in an 18–6 win over Tulane in '94) than the sideline (Alabama went 0–4 in '93).

By '95 Big Little had graduated, and things, to use another oxymoron, got pretty ugly. The Thin Red Line, as 'Bama was known, again lost all four of its games, this time by a com-

HORSING AROUND The 1910 team, with friends.

bined score of 112–12. When Alabama hosted Auburn for the first time in Tuscaloosa, the Red Line was very thin indeed: Auburn won 48–0. A Cadet named Hill Ferguson lamented that "nobody seemed to have enough interest to take a picture of the team."

Abbott begat yet another Quakers alum, Otto Wagonhurst, whose '96 reign spanned just three games and two months. Wagonhurst was supposed to be paid $750, but the senior class, which underwrote his salary, could only come up with $200 after the final game—a 20–0 loss to Mississippi State. The class raised $50 and mailed it to him the next spring. In 1927, after the Crimson Tide had become a national power and won the Rose Bowl, the college's athletic association finally cleared its conscience and cleaned up its books. Wagonhurst was tracked down at an Akron rubber company and paid the remaining $500.

Wagonhurst begat Allen McCants, who won the only game he coached, 6–0 over the Tuscaloosa Athletics. That was also the only game Alabama played in '97. The year before university trustees, concerned over the conflict between athletics and academics, forbade the team from traveling off-campus. Students protested, to no effect. So began the Great Alabama Football Schism, which resulted in no team and no football in '98. Under pressure from students and faculty, the travel ban was lifted in '99, and play resumed.

JOB

After playing against lineman Bully VandeGraaff, Alabama's first All-America, in 1913, Tennessee's Bull Bayer observed, "His ear had a real nasty cut, and it was dangling from his head, bleeding badly. He grabbed his own ear and tried to yank it from his head. His teammates stopped him, and the managers bandaged him. Man, was that guy a tough one. He wanted to tear off his own ear so he could keep playing."

KINGS

Johnny Mack Brown was born in Dothan, Ala., and enrolled at the university in 1922, the year it first gained national prominence by beating Marion (Ala.) Institute 110–0 in the season opener and John Heisman's Pennsyl-

LATE BURST In the post-Thomas era the Tide saw only spotty success; this scamper by Harry Gilmer (52) came in a loss in the 1948 Sugar Bowl.

vania Quakers 9–7 in Philadelphia. A sensational open-field runner dubbed the Dothan Antelope, Brown glided across the gridiron in "low cut" football shoes in an age when players universally wore hightops.

Those shoes were designed by Wallace Wade, the Crimson Tide's first semimythic coach. A perfectionist who used a metronome to hone his players' timing, Wade led the team to the Rose Bowl three times, had three undefeated seasons and won three national championships in his eight years as coach. Brown was the halfback on the unbeaten 1925 squad, which had eight shutouts, outscored its regular-season opponents 297–26 and came from behind to upset Washington 20–19 in the Rose Bowl, the first time a Southern team had been to Pasadena. He caught a couple of TDs on pass plays—one for 58 yards; the other, 62—and was the leading ground-gainer.

Two years later Brown returned to Southern California to become a movie star. He appeared in 167 features—from *Slide, Kelly, Slide* (1927) to *Apache Uprising* ('66) and starred as Billy the Kid in the eponymous film, twirling the real outlaw's six-shooter. Asked what he thought of his star player's acting career, Wade snorted, "He has to make a living doing something."

SONG OF SONGS
Spoiled by success, Tide fans grumbled openly about the 1929 team's disappointing 6–3 record. Angered by the Monday-morning quarterbacking and rumors that his days as coach were numbered, Wade announced that 1930 would be his final year in Tuscaloosa. It was some swan song: After crushing Howard 43–0 in the opener, 'Bama scored 64 points against Ole Miss. During the drubbing, an Atlanta sportswriter heard a fan yell that 'Bama had "the horses." When he heard another fan shout back, "Those aren't horses, they're elephants!" the Tide had a new mascot. Wade's Dumbos scored 271 points to their foes' 13 and—behind the running, passing and kicking of John (Hurri) Cain—capped a 10–0 season by stomping Washington State 24–0 in the Rose Bowl. So confident was Wade of victory that he started his second team. Popular crooner Rudy Vallee dedicated the

ROSY PAST Foots Clement at the 1931 Rose Bowl.

tune *Football Freddie* to tackle Fred Sington, who made All-America and Phi Beta Kappa:

Football Freddie, rugged and tan,
Football Freddie, collegiate man.

NUMBERS
Wade's successor, Frank Thomas, was nearly as successful. During 16 seasons as coach the former Notre Dame quarterback and roommate of Irish immortal George Gipp had a 115-24-7 mark and made three Rose Bowls, winning twice. Among his most luminous stars were quarterback Dixie Howell, receivers Don Hutson and Bear Bryant, and guard Arthur (Tarzan) White, whose biggest fame came as the world's heavyweight wrestling champ. The '34 team was Thomas's best. At a time when scoring was scanty, the Tide averaged 31.6 points a game to its opponents' 4.5. Before a crowd of 84,484, it steamrollered Stanford 29–13 in the Rose Bowl. Howell threw a 59-yard touchdown pass to Hutson but is best remembered for thumbing his nose at Stanford defensive back Buck Van Dellen while sprinting 67 yards into the end zone. Howell insisted he had only been waving. Only his mom believed him.

PROVERBS
Thomas retired after 1946 and named assistant Harold (Red) Drew as his heir. But it wasn't long before the public started doubting Thomas. In '51 the Tide had its first losing season since '03; three years later it had its second. That was evidently one too many for the administration, which moved Drew from football to track. "They said my football team was too slow," he cracked. "So they made me track coach."

The most enduring image from the final days of the B.B. era comes out of the '54 Cotton Bowl, which Alabama lost to Rice 28–6. With Rice ahead 7–6, Owls halfback Dicky Moegle scampered down the sideline, outrunning every Tide defender on his way to a certain 95-yard touchdown. Suddenly Alabama fullback Tommy Lewis, who was watching from the sideline, leaped onto the field and tackled him. "I guess I'm just too full of 'Bama," Lewis more or less explained.

Amen.

POINTS MAN Coach Thomas, left, with captain Bill Lee; their 1934 team outscored opponents by an average of 31.6 to 4.5.

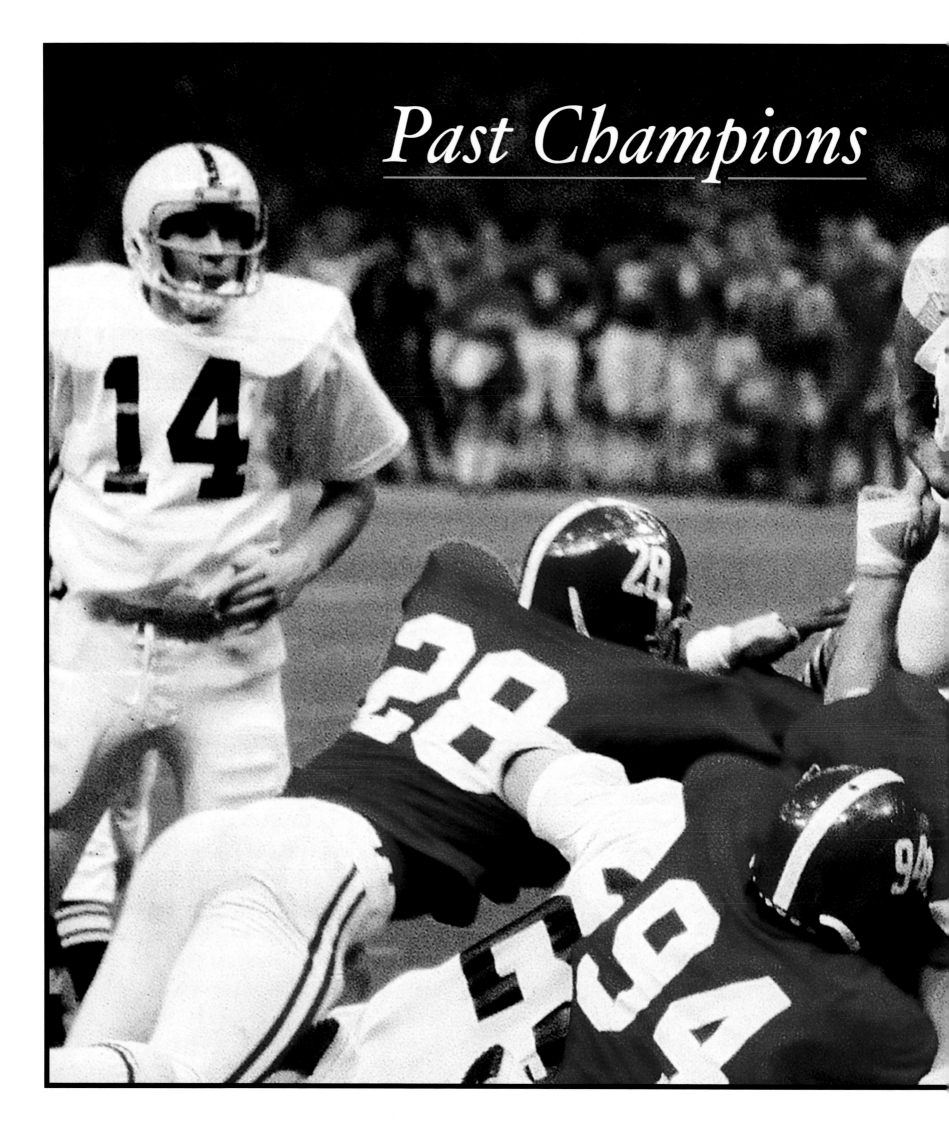

GLORY YEARS

PHOTOGRAPH BY JAMES DRAKE

1978 THE GOAL LINE STAND against Penn State in the Sugar Bowl is one of many moments that elevated the Tide.

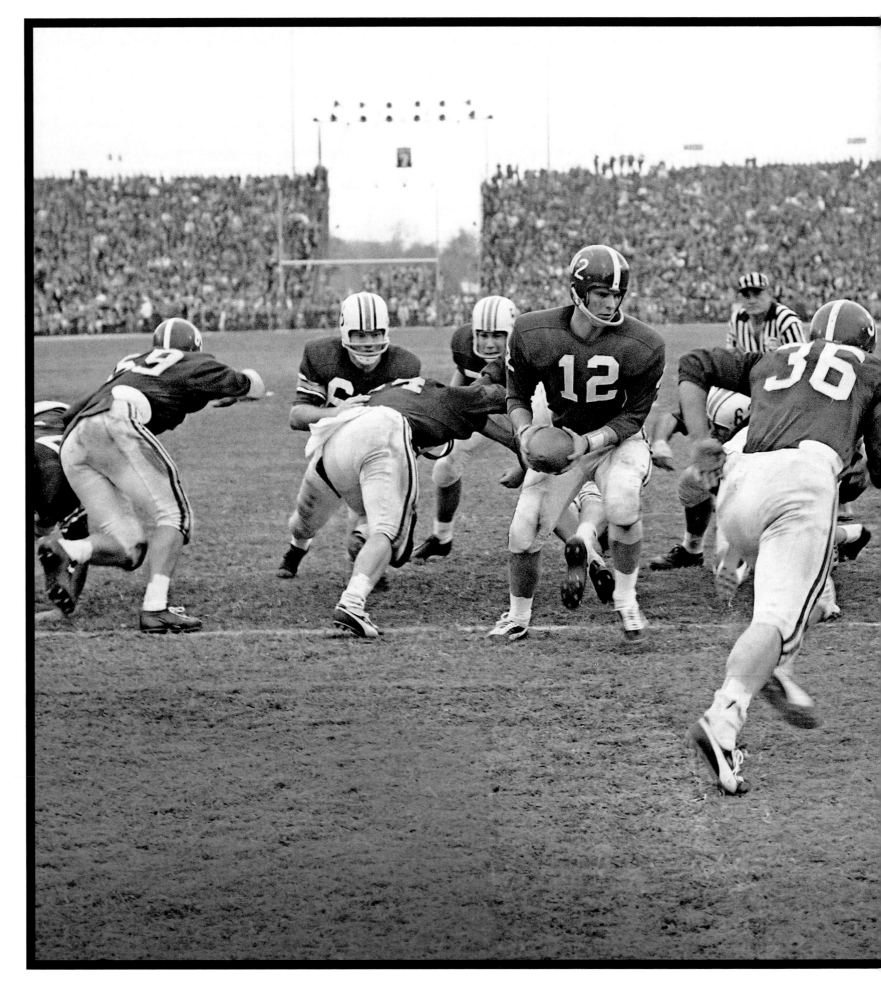

1961

Alabama won titles in 1925, '26, '30, '34 and '41. SI, founded in 1954, first covered a Tide championship team in '61, when 'Bama went 11–0 and earned coach Bear Bryant his first crown.

LESS THAN FIVE MINUTES REMAINED in the ball game, and Alabama was leading 34–0 when Bobby Hunt sent Auburn whirling 65 yards against the 'Bama reserves to a first down in the shadow of the Alabama goal. Bear Bryant, a man who would rather surrender his left lung than a touchdown, sent in the Crimson Tide's first string. Four plays later the Tigers were still in the shadow of the Alabama goal. When the final gun went off a few moments later, its report lost in the frenzy of 54,000 Alabamians whooping onto Legion Field, Bryant permitted himself one of his rare smiles. His Crimson Tide—unbeaten and untied in 10 games, unscored on in the last five, heading for a Sugar Bowl date with Arkansas—had won the national championship just as surely as there is a piece of pig iron in Birmingham.

Alabama won the game on Saturday because it performed on offense as it has seldom performed all year. With quarterback Pat Trammell controlling the ball game, the Tide rolled up 315 yards and 20 first downs. But it also intercepted four passes, recovered the game's only fumble and, in the final analysis, won as it has been winning all year, by sending still another opponent home with knots on its head.

Alabama has allowed just three touchdowns and a total of 22 points. Yet this is not a unit of superstars; the line is almost small by big-time college football standards, and the professional scouts will tell you that there isn't a real standout prospect in the lot. The reason it plays defense so well is because that is the way Bryant asks his team to play, hitting again and again with the viciousness of a pack of sharks until someone goes down.

"I don't know whether that's a great team," said coach Shug Jordan of Auburn after it was all over, "but they were great today. I don't guess anybody has ever hit us quite as hard." When Bear Bryant heard that, he nodded his head.

To Paul William Bryant a fact is a fact, and he is not given to shows of false modesty. If there is a touch of genius about the man, it resides in two areas: organizational talent and the ability to instill a bursting sense of pride in his athletes, enabling boys to play a bruising game as if they were already men. Because of his fierce energy and intelligence and dedication, he has become the best football coach in the land. And that's why, with the possible exception of Oklahoma's Bud Wilkinson, he makes more money than anyone in the business.

Apparently Alabamians don't mind a bit. Just so long as they remain at the top. They're getting to like high living down there.

BY ROY TERRELL | *SI, December* 11, 1961

TIDE ROLLING Trammell, handing the ball off to Larry Wall, directed an Alabama offense that gained 20 first downs and chewed up 315 yards. | *Photograph by* MARVIN E. NEWMAN

IN CHARGE Trammell (12), diving forward, played the game with a poise more typical of professional quarterbacks. | *Photograph by* MARVIN E. NEWMAN

ROUGHED UP After the game Auburn coach Jordan said, "I don't guess anybody has ever hit us quite as hard." | *Photograph by* MARVIN E. NEWMAN

BEARING UP Even before he won this first national championship, Bryant was already a home-state hero. | *Photograph by* MARVIN E. NEWMAN

RUSH DELIVERY Running back Billy Richardson (35) ran in two of Alabama's scores on a day when the ground game dominated. | *Photograph by* MARVIN E. NEWMAN

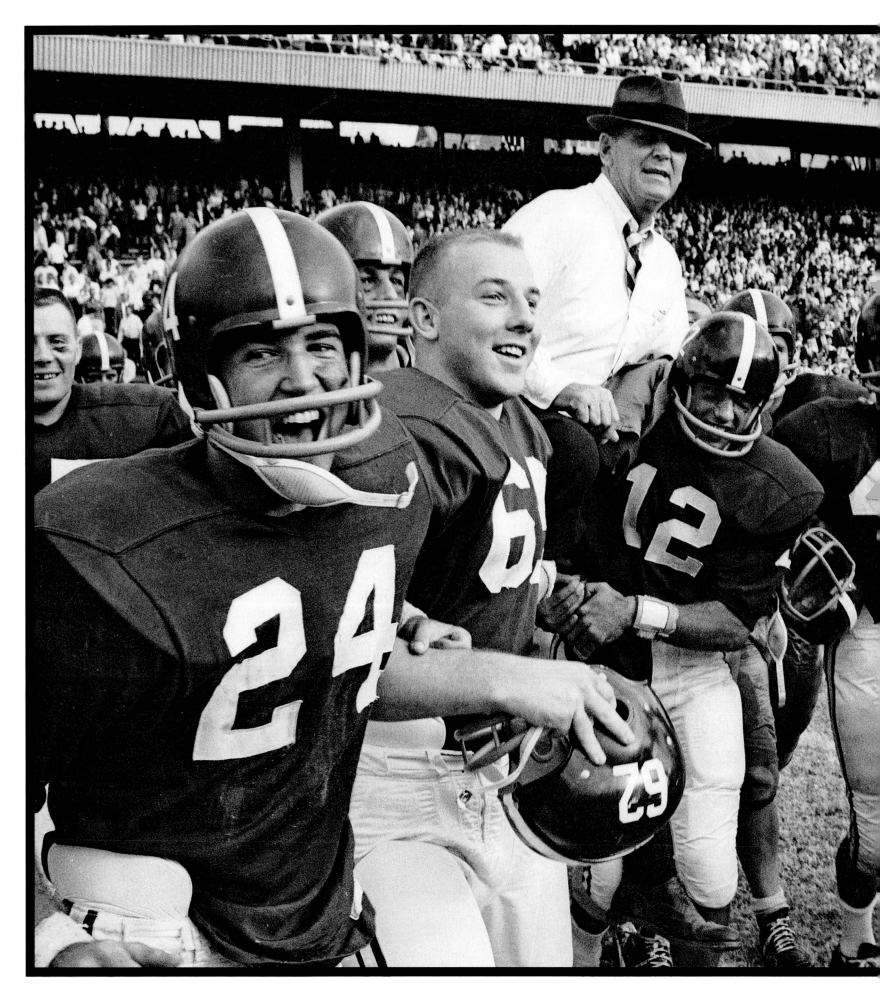

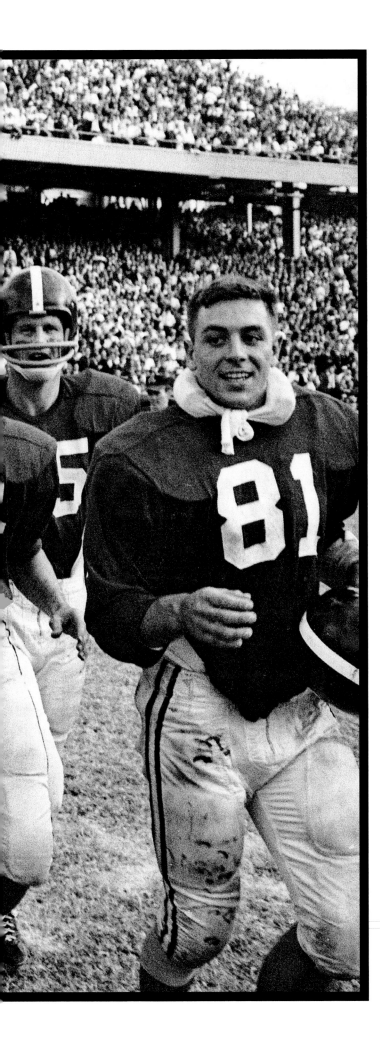

1964

A knee injury kept Joe Namath from starting in a key game, but the senior All-America quarterback was still able to work his magic and win a championship before he left Tuscaloosa.

GIMPY KNEE OR NOT, ALABAMA quarterback Joe Namath has a way of making his presence felt. When a tackler in the Vanderbilt game jeered at him, "Hey, number 12, what's your name?" Namath replied, "You'll see it in the headlines tomorrow." On the next play Namath threw a touchdown pass. Now, at a pep rally on the Thursday before the Crimson Tide was to face Georgia Tech in Atlanta, Namath was addressing the largest crowd of the year in the Alabama gymnasium.

"Two years ago," he said after a long wait for the applause to ebb, "we went to Atlanta. We had won eight straight and were Number 1 in the country. We lost. This year we're 8 and 0, and we're Number 2. Saturday we're going to win in Atlanta, and we're going to come back to the Number 1 university in the country."

Namath's injured knee had not regained enough mobility according to coach Paul (Bear) Bryant, so when the game began, Steve Sloan was at quarterback. Namath stood waiting on the sideline, to be used only when Bryant thought his presence on the field was absolutely necessary.

With less than two minutes to halftime and 'Bama nesting on the Tech 49, Bryant called for Namath, of whom he has said, "I believe Joe can do just about anything." At first Joe did nothing and looked bad doing it. On a straight drop-back pattern he hesitated too long, and his pass was tipped away by a Tech lineman. On second down he pumped twice trying a comeback pass to flanker back Ray Ogden. It was short, and a good thing, too, because Tech's Gerry Bussell almost got to the ball.

The next play was sent in from the bench, but Namath had already called it. Back to Bussell's side, this time to Dave Ray, inserted at flanker in Ogden's place. Namath spiraled the ball into his hands on the run, and Bussell didn't catch him until Ray was on the Tech one-yard line. On the next play fullback Steve Bowman scored.

Tech had barely seen the smoke from the first shot when it was hit with two more. First, end Creed Gilmer recovered Ray's twisting onside kick at the Tech 49. Then Namath passed on first down to Ogden on the right side. Two plays later Namath rolled left and passed to Ray coming left to right in the end zone. The Tide had its second touchdown only a minute and a half after Namath's presence had been deemed absolutely necessary. The effect was devastating and finishing.

In analysis, there was no great inequality of players, despite the protestations of both coaches, except for the 1½ minutes when Alabama had Namath on the field.

BY JOHN UNDERWOOD | *SI, November 23, 1964*

SUPPORT GROUP Namath (12) had an injured knee, but he was tough enough to make plays in spots against Georgia Tech, and to give his coach a celebratory lift. | *Photograph by* JAMES DRAKE

MOTIVATIONAL SPEAKER A player said Namath's pep-rally talk before the Georgia Tech game sent shivers down his spine. | *Photograph by* JAMES DRAKE

STARTING TIMBER Sloan, the backup pressed into action, had his own enthusiasts: At the rally fans shouted, "Steve Sloan for President." | *Photograph by* JAMES DRAKE

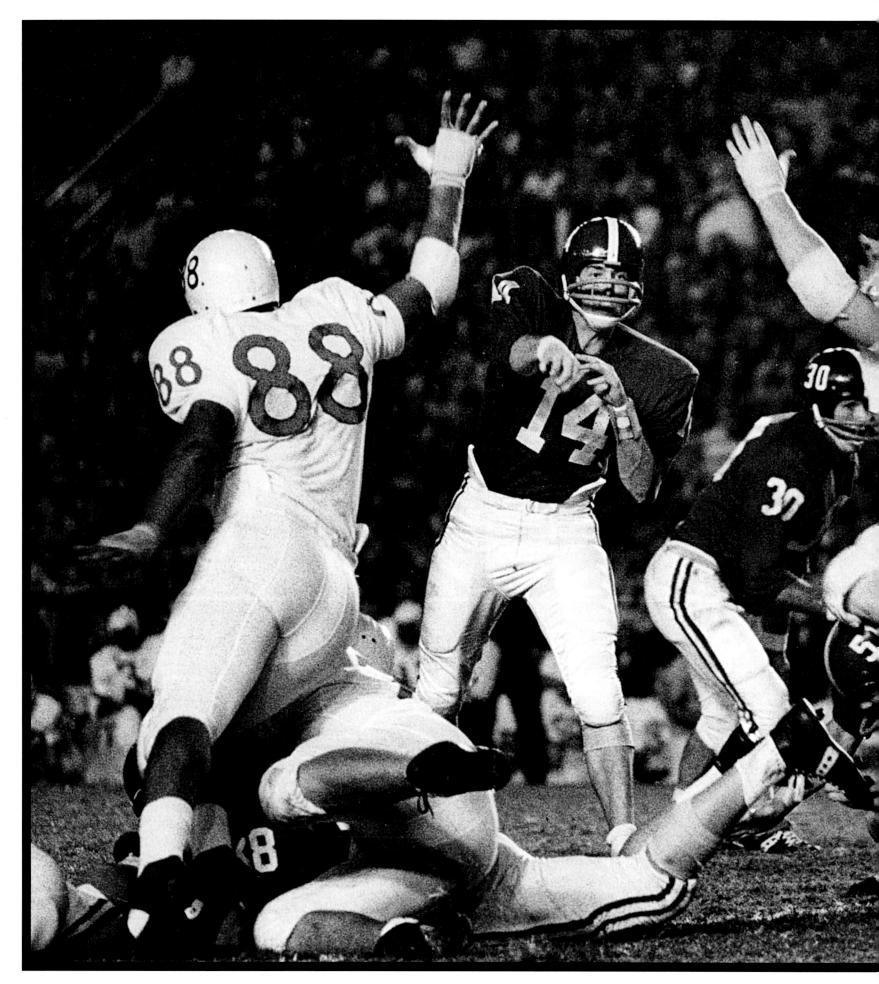

1965

*The Tide took back-to-back championships with Steve Sloan,
now himself an All-America quarterback, directing
an upset of undefeated Nebraska in the Orange Bowl.*

L EADING UP TO THE ORANGE BOWL, much had been said about the contingencies of this classic match—Nebraska's big slugger of an offense against the cunning and dash of the smaller, tougher Bear Bryant Alabama team. On a glittering, perfectly splendid New Year's night, they faced off to determine who would be national champion.

As it turned out, the Cornhuskers scored more points on the Tide than had any other team in Bryant's eight years at the school. But what is the use of scoring 28 points when the other team scores 39? The little giants that operate in the Alabama line move people. It was inconceivable, perhaps, that center Paul Crane at 191 pounds could handle Nebraska's middle guard, 239-pound Wayne Meylan, but Crane did it with regularity. Not with brute force, by any means. 'Bama linemen block at fine angles, aiming for the outside of a knee or a piece of a hip.

More important, Alabama linemen use the impetus of a charging opponent to turn him away from the play. The hole, therefore, might change in a flicker, and the Tide's backs—Steve Bowman, Leslie Kelley and Frank Canterbury—are excellent at cutting back to take advantage. They outrushed the Cornhuskers, the rushing team, 222 yards to 145, and then Alabama threw everything at Nebraska, including three tackle-eligible passes to a former fullback, Jerry Duncan. Three times Bryant ordered onside kicks after touchdowns, and twice the Tide successfully recovered.

The magnificence of the Alabama offense is in its passing game, and that means quarterback Steve Sloan and half a dozen excellent receivers. Almost deferentially, Sloan has gone about wiping out Joe Namath's 'Bama passing records: He had 20 completions for 296 yards, despite having to throw in the face of a persistent Cornhuskers rush and despite playing from the second quarter with torn cartilage in his right side. Unable to follow through completely, Sloan tended to loft the ball, but when he did so, his astoundingly quick receivers were almost always there, curling back or stretching out to make the catch.

Most of the stretching and curling was done by Ray Perkins, who caught 10 passes against Nebraska for 159 yards, including two for touchdowns. Possibly the only thing more spectacular than Perkins's touchdown catches was the chain reaction they set off in the Orange Bowl's east end zone. Touchdowns there were the signals for soaring rockets and Roman candles, lighting up the Miami sky. To have all that and the Alabama offense too was really having all that heaven should allow.

—from SI, January 10, 1966

ARMS CONTROL Leading the offensive onslaught, Sloan had 296 yards passing, including two touchdowns to Perkins. | *Photograph by* PAUL W. BRYANT MUSEUM/UNIVERSITY OF ALABAMA

WRAP ARTIST Jackie Sherrill (36) went high while Tim Bates (56) got 'em low in the '65 Iron Bowl. | *Photograph by* JAY LEVITON/ATLANTA

HIGH TIMES Leslie Kelley (32) contributed a two-yard touchdown in 'Bama's 30–3 win over Auburn. | *Photograph by* JAY LEVITON/ATLANTA

SNAKE BITE Though just a sophomore backup, Kenny Stabler (12) got a taste of the Iron Bowl action. | *Photograph by* JAY LEVITON/ATLANTA

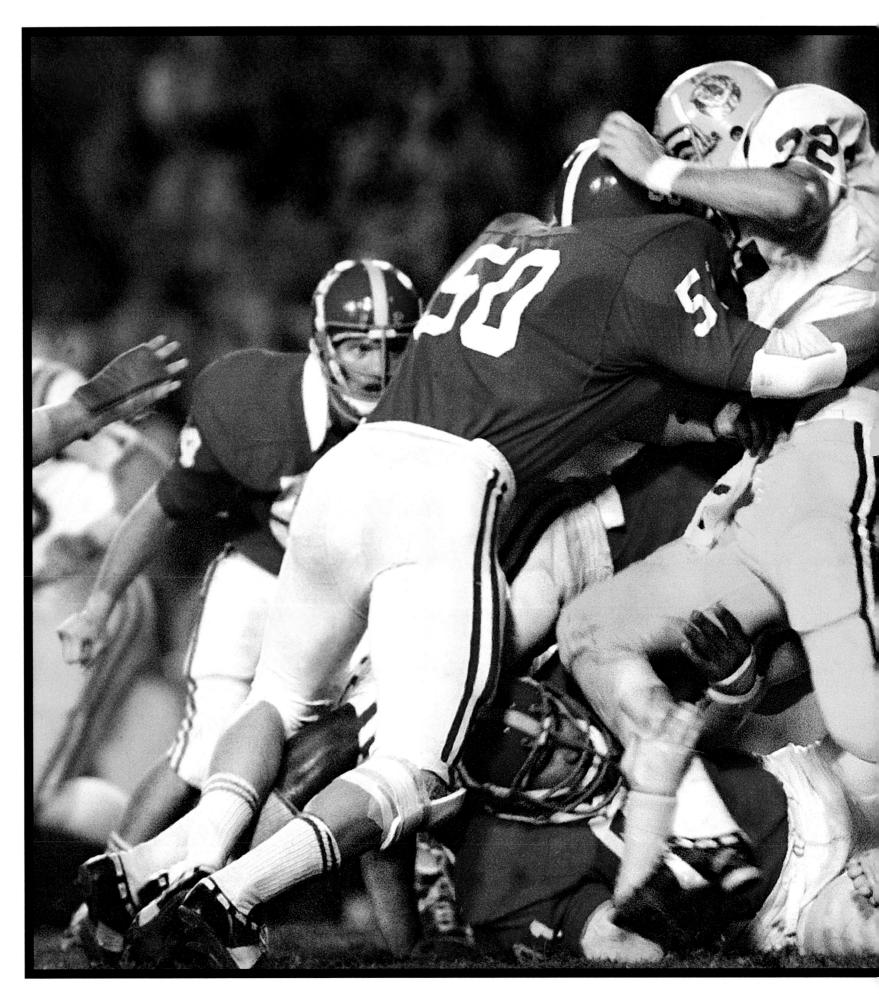

1973

With Bear Bryant's late season 21–7 defeat of one of his disciples, LSU coach Charlie McClendon, Alabama elevated itself to its finishing spot at the top of the polls.

O N A THANKSGIVING WEEKEND that served up a cornucopia of significant college football action—four games featuring matchups of Top 10 teams—the most compelling confrontation was between No. 2 Alabama and No. 7 LSU. Bear Bryant brought the Crimson Tide to Baton Rouge, and the mist had barely settled on the bayous when he and LSU's Charlie McClendon were bragging on one another again. It is a gracious Southern ritual that has been going on since McClendon, who is not only a fellow traveler from Arkansas but also played and coached under Bryant, took over at LSU in 1962.

According to the script Bryant puts on his most venerable face and then says, as he did last week, "Cholly Mac and I are good friends, as everyone knows, and I hope he'll be kind to his old coach." Then, after Bryant's boys waylay McClendon's, as they have done seven times in nine games, Cholly Mac will drawl, "Somehow I don't think Bear taught me all he knows."

There were hints of that last week when Bryant prophesied that "mistakes will decide this game." Collaring the referees before the game, the coach tried to make certain that his young squad would not be rattled by Tiger Stadium, a notorious arena that has justifiably been dubbed Death Valley. With the Southeastern Conference title at stake and both teams flaunting unblemished records, the playing conditions were, as one 'Bama player described them, "downright hellacious."

It was Alabama, however, that took the Tigers by the tail in the first half. The Tide—one of the top 10 teams in scoring, rushing, total offense and total defense—must also lead in the unofficial category of total depth. Shuttling 70 or more players into each game, Bryant this year has achieved a battering effect on opposing teams.

After LSU held Alabama to a standoff in the first period, a Tigers handoff went astray and 'Bama tackle Mike Raines pounced on the ball at the LSU 19. Then quarterback Gary Rutledge made a fake into the line and peeled off on a keeper to score easily. Minutes later Rutledge flipped a pass to a very lonely tight end, George Pugh, who loped in for a 49-yard score. LSU's last critical error came in the third quarter when Tigers cornerback Mike Williams fell while covering the Tide's Wayne Wheeler, and the fleet split end easily turned the play into a 77-yard TD.

Afterward Bryant and McClendon slipped back into their routine. "I'm tickled to death to win from Cholly Mac," said the Bear. "He's taught me a lot. I always try to learn from my best boys."

BY RAY KENNEDY | *SI, December 3, 1973*

REAL HANDFUL Linebacker Wayne Hall (50) and the 'Bama defense forced the Tigers into five turnovers—three interceptions and two fumbles. | *Photograph by* NEIL LEIFER

FAMILIAR FOE Bryant gave a warm greeting to former player McClendon—or, as Bear called him, Cholly Mac. | *Photograph by* NEIL LEIFER

DOUBLE TROUBLE Rutledge (11) contributed to the scoring with a 19-yard run and pass plays of 49 and 77 yards. | *Photograph by* NEIL LEIFER

1978

Alabama's 14–7 win over Penn State in the Sugar Bowl is remembered for its goal line stand, a signature moment that capped the Tide's dominating defensive effort.

O N THE DAY BEFORE HIS SUGAR BOWL showdown with Penn State, Bear Bryant breakfasted in his hotel suite high above New Orleans on an egg-and-bacon sandwich and coffee in a Styrofoam cup. Between swallows the Bear said that if there was one thing you could be sure of about his Alabama defense, it was that you couldn't be sure of his Alabama defense. It had been great at times and unsound at times, and that's "not recommended" when you play the No. 1 team in the nation, one that had not lost in 19 games.

Bear noted that the Tide defense had been hurt a lot. That it had been particularly slowed in the secondary by those injuries and by, well, being slow in the secondary. And that it was about to go under the gun against a quarterback, Chuck Fusina, whom Penn State coach Joe Paterno called the best passer he's ever had. The situation fairly cried out for a dedicated pass rush, and "rushing the passer is the thing we do worst," said Bryant.

As for the Alabama fans who were establishing themselves as No. 1 in whoops and hollers on Bourbon Street, Bryant said he wished they'd be quiet until after the game.

Well, Bear, you can come down now and join the party. And bring the defense with you. On second thought, have them bring you.

In as thorough a demonstration of defensive scratch-and-harry as you'll ever see, the Tide not only shut Fusina down, but it also rushed him to distraction. The result was a 14–7 Alabama victory that should bring Bryant a fifth national title.

The stunting, blitzing Alabama defenders suffocated the Penn State running game, holding the Nittany Lions to a net +19 yards overall. Ends Wayne Hamilton and E.J. Junior, tackles Marty Lyons and Byron Braggs, middle guard Curtis McGriff and linebackers Rickey Gilliland and Barry Krauss took turns stuffing runners like sausages. When Fusina tried to pass, these same gentlemen generally clogged his sinuses and sacked him five times for a total loss of 70 yards. When he did get the ball upfield, there was that slow, small and underesteemed secondary of Don McNeal, Allen Crumbley, Murray Legg and Jim Bob Harris picking off passes, four in all. Then in the fourth quarter a rocklike goal line stand (in which Krauss was briefly knocked cold) stopped Penn State on the one-foot line, and the Lions never threatened again.

Bryant said afterward that Alabama "could have beaten any team in the country" that day. The Bear went on to say that he could not recall ever being prouder of a team, and if they wanted his vote for No. 1, they had it.

BY JOHN UNDERWOOD | *SI, January 8, 1979*

STANDUP GUYS Alabama stopped Penn State tailback Mike Guman on fourth down from the one; the previous play the defense had stuffed fullback Matt Suhey. | *Photograph by* WALTER IOOSS JR.

TITANIC CLASH In this meeting with future alltime wins leader Joe Paterno, the Bear walked off victorious. | *Photograph by* JOHN IACONO

RED BLANKET The Tide forced four interceptions, including this one by McNeal (28) in the end zone. | *Photograph by* WALTER IOOSS JR.

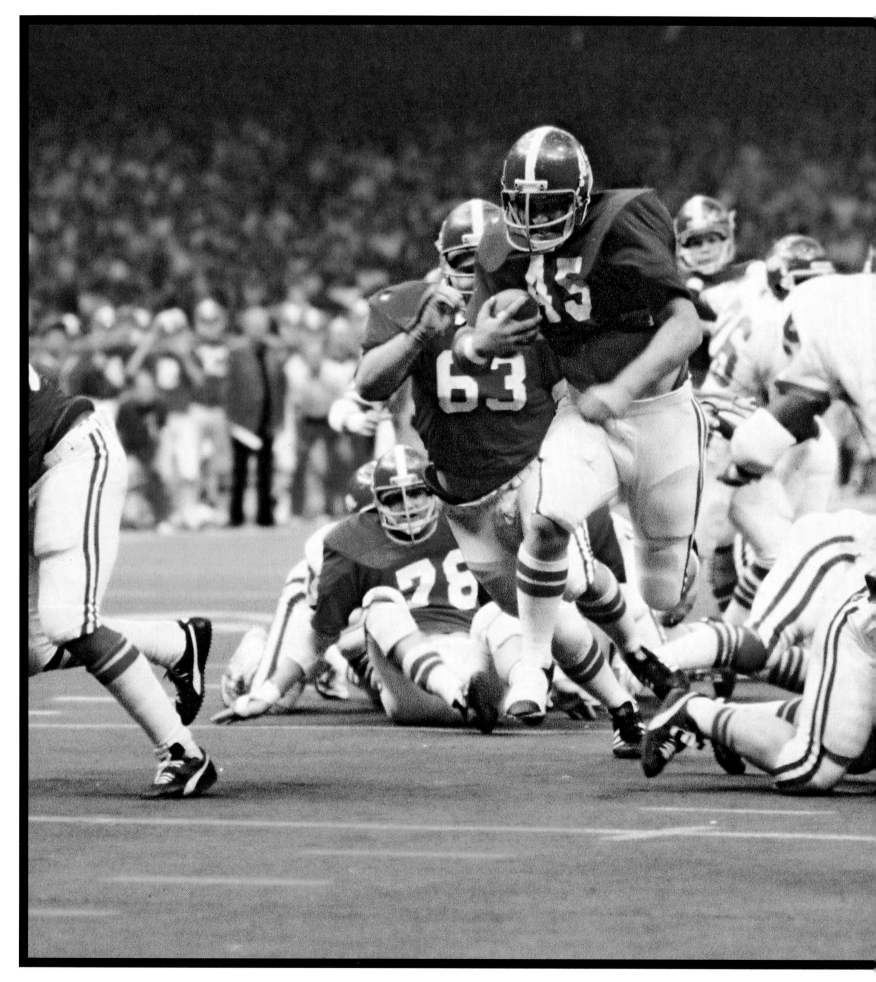

1979

Alabama's Sugar Bowl win and its aftermath provides a window into how national titles were decided in the days before the Bowl Championship Series.

SHORTLY AFTER QUARTERBACKING Alabama to its 24–9 Sugar Bowl victory over Arkansas, Steadman Shealy lay sprawled across a bed in the Hyatt Regency in New Orleans watching Ohio State and USC in the Rose Bowl. Crowded around him were his mother, father, girlfriend, sister and brother-in-law. Mainly, the room was quiet. But late in the game, when USC's Charles White dived over the goal line to tie the game at 16, Shealy leaped to his feet. "Whooeee!" he shouted. "Now, miss the extra point! No, wait! I don't know! Is that good? Or bad?"

Normally Shealy is not one to be confused. An education major, he ranks in the top 1% of his class. But in his two previous seasons at Alabama, the Tide had scored big Sugar Bowl wins and a shot at the national championship. In 1977 AP's poll of sports-writers and UPI's poll of college coaches had dashed Shealy's hopes. A year ago, when 'Bama upset No. 1–ranked Penn State, it got the AP's No. 1 spot but not UPI's. Now another national title was up to the voters, and the other two finalists were in the Rose Bowl. "Who knows what those people are thinking," said Shealy.

At the moment they had to be thinking Alabama. Before a record 77,486 in the Superdome, the Tide had gripped a highly talented sixth-ranked Arkansas team by the lapels and never let go. In the first half the Razorbacks faced six third downs, and on those six critical plays the Hogs' net gain was zero. At halftime the Tide led 17–3. By then, too, Alabama's Major Ogilvie had two touchdowns, returned a punt 50 yards and nailed down the MVP award.

But what crushed Arkansas was the performance of Don McNeal, Byron Braggs, E.J. Junior and the rest of 'Bama's defense, which had given up an average of just five points per game in 1979. Although the Hogs' Kevin Scanlon completed 22 of 39 passes, he was left on his feet after only two of those throws.

Back at the Hyatt, as Shealy and his family took in the closing seconds of the Rose Bowl, a final crisis for Alabama suddenly arose. Leading 17–16, USC took possession on the Buckeyes' 20 and was in position to score. Another touchdown would mean an eight-point win, which just might swing some AP and UPI votes. But the clock ran out with USC on the four. "Perfect!" screamed Shealy's mother, Peggy.

With classes out at Tuscaloosa, Shealy and his girlfriend drove to his grandmother's house in Madison, Miss. The next night he got the word: Alabama was No. 1 in both polls, with USC second. "It's joyous," Shealy said. "Praise the Lord!" And Ogilvie and a defense that impressed even the pollsters.

BY MIKE DeLNAGRO | *SI, January* 14, 1980

DEAL SEALER Steve Whitman's 12-yard touchdown run in the fourth quarter capped a 98-yard drive and also the scoring in the Crimson Tide's 24–9 win. | *Photograph by* HEINZ KLUETMEIER

PITCHING IN In a game in which Alabama ran for 284 yards and passed for 70, wishbone quarterback Shealy's role was clear. | *Photograph by* RICH CLARKSON

ANOTHER D DAY Bobby Smith and the defense, which had allowed five points per regular-season game, was as stingy as ever against Arkansas. | *Photograph by* RICH CLARKSON

1992

Behind a defense led by All-Americas John Copeland, Eric Curry and Antonio Langham, the Tide ran the table, capping an undefeated season by knocking off Miami 34–13 in the Sugar Bowl.

DESPITE ALABAMA COACH GENE Stallings' stubborn refusal in the days leading up to the Sugar Bowl to concede that his team was an underdog, the Crimson Tide's 34–13 win on New Year's Day over the defending national champion Miami Hurricanes was an upset of magnificent proportions. Alabama quarterback Jay Barker could not be counted on to pass his team to victory. Likewise, the outside running game would be an exercise in futility. The Crimson Tide would have to run between the tackles—football's truck route—behind a smallish, undistinguished line that 'Bama fans had maligned. At 6' 3" and 250 pounds, center Tobie Sheils is slight for a major-college lineman. Left guard George Wilson shot off half of his left foot in a 1989 hunting accident. And six nights before the game right tackle Roosevelt Patterson was verbally assaulted in the French Quarter. "You must be an offensive lineman, you fat, sloppy [expletive]," Miami linebacker Rohan Marley had shouted at the amply padded, 290-pound Patterson. Chalk one up for the shrimp, the gimp and the blimp. Behind them Derrick Lassic rushed for 135 yards on 28 carries, the most yards a back gained against the Hurricanes this season.

When Miami had the ball, on several occasions Alabama placed 11 men on the line of scrimmage. It was a naked challenge to quarterback Gino Torretta: Beat us deep if you can. The outcome was a pick party. Torretta threw three interceptions, each of which led, directly or indirectly, to a Crimson Tide touchdown.

George Teague returned one of those picks for a touchdown, and then the safety outdid himself with slightly more than nine minutes left in the third quarter. Miami faced second-and-10 at its own 11-yard line. Senior wideout Lamar Thomas had burst past cornerback Willie Gaston and hauled in Torretta's sweetest pass of the evening at the Hurricanes' 36. Thomas was headed for the goal line. As he neared the end zone, however, a crimson blur rapidly closed on him. "I was supposed to be behind him," said Teague. "If I didn't catch him, I was going to be in trouble."

Teague caught Thomas at the Crimson Tide 15, but he was not content to make a tackle. Reaching over Thomas's right shoulder with his right hand, he wrested the ball from Thomas, thereby effecting the most remarkable full-gallop fumble recovery in memory.

Three coaches and one decade to the month after the death of Bear Bryant, Alabama won its first national title in 13 years.

BY AUSTIN MURPHY | *SI, January* 11, 1993

U TURN Miami players doubted Alabama could move the ball on the Hurricanes' defense, but Lassic and friends proved otherwise. | *Photograph by* RICHARD MACKSON

STING TRIO Miami quarterback Torretta, the 1992 Heisman winner, was harassed into throwing three interceptions. | *Photograph by* PETER READ MILLER

RUNBACK KID This 31-yard interception return by Teague (13) put Alabama up 27–6 in the third quarter. | *Photograph by* PETER READ MILLER

CARRYING CHARGES A decade after the Bear retired, 'Bama had a new leader to lionize in Gene Stallings. | *Photograph by* JOHN BIEVER

RUNNING TALLY Lassic's 135 yards were the most any back gained on Miami's vaunted defense that season. | *Photograph by* AL TIELEMANS

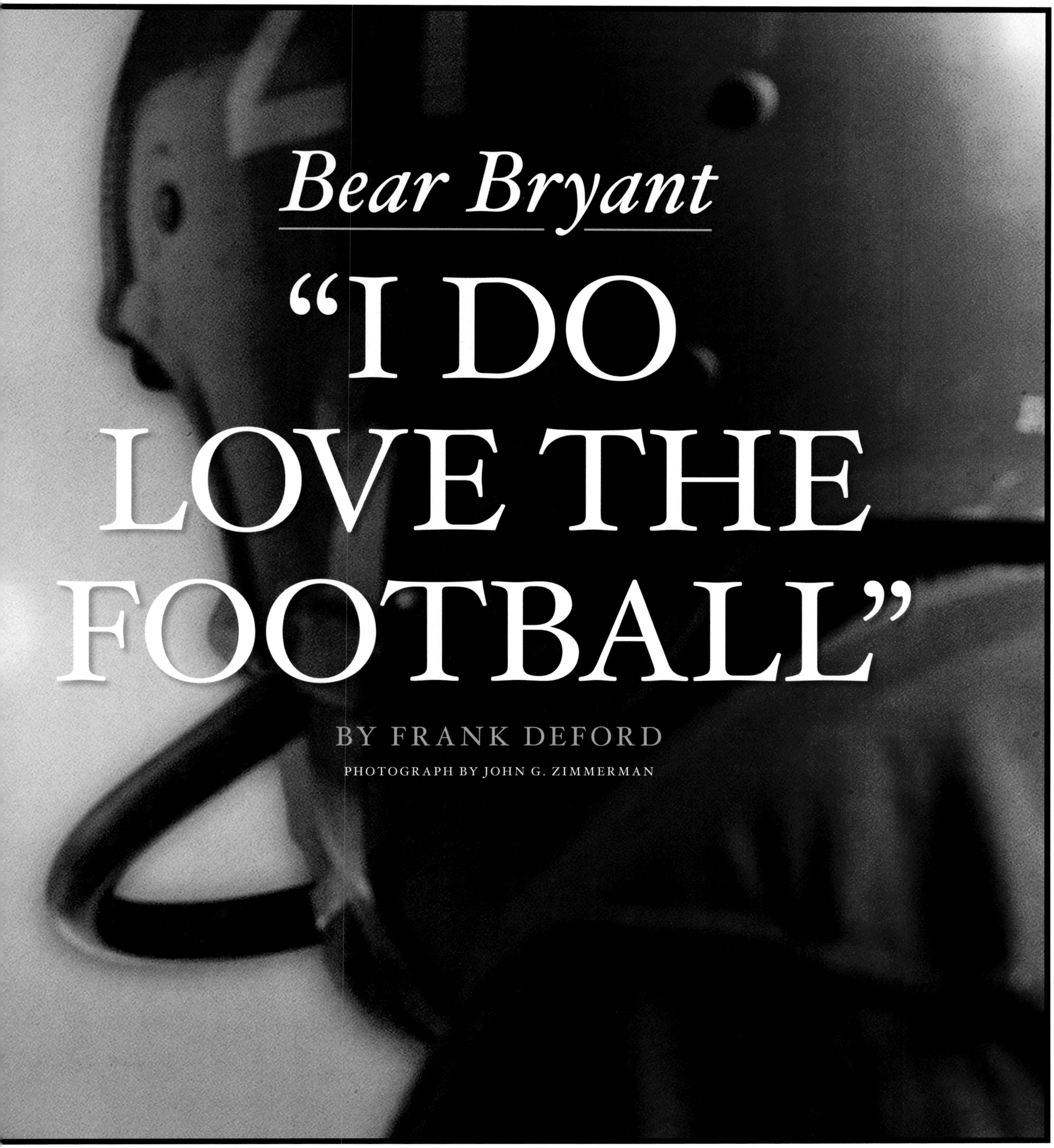

Bear Bryant

"I DO LOVE THE FOOTBALL"

BY FRANK DEFORD

PHOTOGRAPH BY JOHN G. ZIMMERMAN

As Bear Bryant neared the alltime wins record for coaches, Frank Deford wrote this defining profile of the man and his place in Alabama lore. —*from* SI, NOVEMBER 23, 1981

THE PIGSKIN HISTORIAN begins to sort through the mounds of evidence that are supposed to add up to the man who is identified as coach Paul (Bear) Bryant. It is all there, in layers, by now a folk chronicle, each tale told and retold in nearly the same language every time, and all irrespective of relative importance, time or place: the Bear and his humble origins in Moro Bottom, near Fordyce, Ark.; the Bear at Alabama as "the other end" opposite the immortal Don Hutson; the tales of how the Bear got his name (accounts provided by every possible eyewitness, save perhaps the noble ursine itself); the Bear and the bowls; the Bear and the record—Amos Alonzo Stagg's 314 victories as a coach, which Bryant tied last Saturday with a 31–16 defeat of Penn State and could surpass next week against Auburn; the Bear that first hellish summer in Aggieland; the Bear returns to his Alabama; the Bear and his hat; the Bear and the Baron; the Bear walks on water (and other fables); the ages of the Bear.

By now it is all so blurred, yet all so neat. The more one reads—the more one suffers through the same stuff from the Bear and his hagiographers—the more one understands a friend of the Bear's, a Tuscaloosa physician, who says, "That he mumbles really doesn't matter to me anymore, because by now, I always know what he is going to say, anyway."

But, what have we here? Tucked deep into the recesses of another bio folder, there is one other obscure clipping, from a time long ago. It seems, studying this scrap of parchment, that as yet another Honor America Day approached, a certain U.S. politician named Nixon was beleaguered, beset on all sides by his bloodthirsty foes. But after months of holing up, he decided that Honor America Day would be an appropriate occasion on which to launch a counterattack, to venture out again and reach for the souls of decent citizens. And so, he would go forth and deliver a speech.

And here, from *The New York Times*, is the last paragraph of that story: "Invitations to attend the celebration were also sent to John Wayne, the actor; Paul Harvey, the news broadcaster; Billy Graham, the evangelist; and Paul (Bear) Bryant, the University of Alabama football coach."

At that time, the Bear had 231 wins, and was counting.

THE FIRST OF THE TWO-A-DAYS IN THE 24TH year of coach Paul (Bear) Bryant's tenure at Alabama takes place just after dawn on a steamy summer's day, Monday, Aug. 17. It would be winter, 4½ months later, before the Crim-son Tide would be finished playing; the team has gone to a bowl for 22 straight years and, by now, as the Bear says, "We win two games, *some* bowl will invite us." Oddly, he overslept this morning. You'd have thought the Bear would have been raring to go, he being a legend in his own time, this being the start of his supreme season; besides, he's an early riser. But Billy Varner had to rouse him, up at his house by the third green at the Indian Hills Country Club.

Billy drives the Bear around in a Buick LeSabre. He has for six years, since, the Bear explains, "I started gettin' death threats and all kinda things." Billy was a bartender out at the club, and the Bear had him taught to shoot a pistol so he could pass the police tests. They get along beautifully, which is important, because by now the Bear probably spends more time with Billy Varner than he does with his wife, whose name is Mary Harmon if you know the Bear and Miz Bryant if you only worship from afar.

But even with the late start, it wasn't yet six o'clock when Billy got the Bear to his office before the first of the two-a-days. The moon was still up, nearly full, shining through the misty Alabama heavens. The birds were chirping, and about all there was on the roads were milk trucks. They still make milk deliveries mornings in Tuscaloosa.

The players started arriving around 6:30, driving the half mile or so from their private dormitory, Bryant Hall (of course). It was a showpiece when it was built in 1963, but is now more a garish curiosity, with a hideous interior of silver, red and white and a two-tiered fountain outside, which is supported by statues of naked men, their genitalia covered by decorous shields so as not to offend the eyes of innocent 'Bama belles. But then, little of the campus offers much in the way of beauty. The Yankees, it seems, burnt the best of it to the ground just before Appomattox, and what has risen from the ashes is largely without architectural grace. Football constitutes grace in this neck of the woods.

Where the Bear now has his football offices, in Memorial Coliseum, adjoining the practice complex, was all cotton fields when he first arrived in Tuscaloosa, coming over from the bottom country of Arkansas. It was the fall of '31, the Depression, and the segregated South was like a different nation then—one party, one crop, one sport and one dollar if you were lucky. "There wasn't but about three cars on campus then," the Bear recalls, exaggerating only a little bit. Now, as dawn breaks, his players drive up in all manner of vehicles; hardly a one walks the half mile from the dormitory.

The Bear meets briefly with his team—alone. "You wouldn't want someone else to sit in when you talked private with your wife, would you?" he says. Occasionally, he drives home this point in somewhat earthier terms. He's still very close to his boys. He doesn't sleep over at the dormitory anymore, the way Joe Namath remembers, but there is still a tight bond.

THE PLAYER Before he became a coaching legend, Bryant played end for Alabama teams that went 23-3-2 over three seasons and topped several polls in 1934.

"I get so tired of it at times," the Bear admits, "but I do love the football, the contact with my players. I still get a *thrill* outta jes goin' to practice. Jes steppin' out there. I do. That's my hobby." Another thing he says, regularly, when strangers ask even innocuous questions about his players, is this: "I wouldn't know, and I wouldn't tell you if I did."

The Bear puts on his baseball cap now, for practice. He is about the last man who has his hair and still wears a hat all the time. Outside of coach Paul (Bear) Bryant down in Alabama, you can tell bald men this way: They are the ones in hats. But if the Bear still has hair, it isn't so curly and bright as it used to be, so his jug ears stand out more. In fact he can look very old sometimes, away from the sideline stripes. He is wrinkled and gray and his coat rides up high on his neck and his pants droop off his seat, and he just shuffles along. He looks, for example, a lot older than the President, who is, at 70, 2½ years his senior. "Yeah, but the President ain't run around and drank anywhere near so much whiskey as the Bear," a friend says. That's probably true, although not necessarily to the benefit of the ship of state.

"My doctor says I look 10 years younger than last year," the Bear was mumbling the other day when Billy drove him up to Birmingham for a luncheon at a hotel. He growls so low and so slow that when he made a commercial for Ford trucks not long ago, they had to speed up the sound track so Americans at home would understand it was Ford trucks he was extolling. "Ten years," the Bear went on. "Of course, in the first place he's lying, and in the second, there's all these pills—11 in the morning, alone. Why, I'm plain goofy now." And he was, for a time. Also, like a lot of old men, he has weak kidneys. "Billy, have I passed all my pissin' places?" the Bear asked, as they neared Birmingham. They had, so at the hotel, people followed him right to the men's room. But the Bear never slights anybody if he can help it. When he greets someone, he keeps an arm around him, or, even after the handshake, he holds onto him by the wrist or forearm, as if momentarily he is going to send him into a huddle.

But now, the moon is gone, the sun is up for the first of the two-a-days, and the Bear strides through the guarded tunnel that goes from the coliseum to the practice fields, under a fence topped with barbed wire and masked with high shrubs.

LITTLE BEAR Bryant (first row, far left) with his family in 1915.

And now the Bear is different. He is some kind of different. He is coach Paul (Bear) Bryant, and he seems an altogether new man, a whole lot younger. He puts out his cigarette and climbs into his golf cart and drives off toward his tower, which is celebrated this way in one of the ballads about him:

His reign of power
From his tower,
Bear Bryant,
The Gridiron King.

The ground has turned two shades of green by now, lighter where many footprints and one set of golf cart tracks have cut through the wet grass. It's likely to be more humid early in the day, when the dew is lifting, so the players are made to stop and rest regularly on one knee, with their helmets off, and receive liquids. They kneel all in one straight line, served by managers, so that it looks exactly like some huge open-air communion. "All right, all right," hollers the Bear. "Not all slouched up like a bunch of idiots."

Once, years ago, his players practiced till they dropped— literally. It's amazing someone didn't die when the Bear was coaching back there at Texas A&M. If you took off your helmet or needed water, you were just a damn old sissy. But now, here the Bear is, making sure they all drink exactly the proper amount of liquid and let their heads cool off.

("You see, Coach Bryant was always very good at adjusting," Bud Wilkinson says. Wilkinson had 145 victories when he packed it in at Oklahoma in 1963 to run for the Senate. Why, he could be past 315 by now if he had stuck with it. Add it up for yourself. "The main thing about staying a coach so long is that you've got to want to," Wilkinson says.)

A freight train rumbles by, just as practice is ready to start. And suddenly, for no reason, the Bear starts to sing. "Love lifted me!" he sings. Well, it's more of a holler. And then again, the refrain from the old hymn: "Love lif . . . i . . . ted me!" Nobody ventures to ask the Bear why he has chosen this song here at the start of the two-a-days.

Now he begins to trudge up the 33 steps to the top of the tower, where a chair, a bullhorn and a can of bug spray await him. The latter is for some hornets up there who don't

BROADWAY REHEARSAL Bryant with Namath (12) in 1964, the year the coach and the quarterback paired for a national title.

appreciate what place the man in the tower holds in the human kingdom. He peers down on all his players. There are almost 130, counting the walk-ons, all in color-coded shirts—red for the first offense, white for first defense, blue, green, yellow and orange—looking like game pieces on some great, green, white-striped board. The Gridiron King will zero in on this one or that one for two or three plays, but, of course, nobody down there knows whom he might be watching at any given moment. He'll just all of a sudden yell out, "Nice catch" or "Straight up, straight up" or "You can't run any faster than that, get your ass outta here" or "Come on, come on, start showin' some class. Fourth quarter now, fourth quarter." But everybody feels the Bear is coming right down on him, which is the way he wants it.

The Bear says, "When I first came here I was fightin' for my life out there on the field. Well, I'm still fightin' for my life. It's just that I don't have near as many years left." It is only at the very end of the second session of the opening two-a-days that the Bear lets himself lounge back in his chair. Then he just sits up there for a while, the pink twilight over his shoulder, watching the last of the maneuvers below. It's past 7 p.m. before he starts down the tower for the last time. "They were comin' off the ball pretty good," the Bear allows. Better be; there are barely two weeks left till the opener over in Baton Rouge, against LSU. That will be number 307.

OTHER END Bryant (left) played opposite Hutson.

BY THE TIME COACH PAUL (BEAR) Bryant got back to Alabama, age 44, in 1958, he had already accumulated 91 coaching victories at Maryland, Kentucky and Texas A&M, places on the fringes of Dixie. Now he was returning to his alma mater, to home, and in the very year that C. Vann Woodward, the distinguished Southern historian, was making this observation: "The time is coming, if indeed it has not already arrived, when the Southerner will begin to ask himself whether there is really any longer very much point in calling himself a Southerner." How could C. Vann Woodward

know that, 23 years later, the Bear would be going for 315?

The Bear is meaningful. That is his legacy—not just so many more victories. History has always been important to the South, and the Bear is a historical figure. It was right after another victory last month, number 310, and Billy had just driven him away in the Buick LeSabre, two motorcycle cops running ahead through the traffic, their blue lights flashing, when someone was moved to say, "They'll sure never be another Bear." And the writer from the campus newspaper, an Alabama boy, said, "Well, not unless there's another Civil War."

And that is pretty much it. For Alabama, anyway, the Bear is triumph, at last; even more than that, he is justification.

The Bear hates all that joking about him being some sort of Dixie Christ (his card-playing friends back at Indian Hills refer to him as Old Water Walker—behind his back), and he's right to, for whether or not it's sacrilege, it's bad theology. The Bear is very human. That is the point. He is one of their own good old boys who took on the rest of the nation and whipped it. The wisest thing that the Bear never did was to run against George Wallace for governor, not so much because he probably would have lost and that would have burst his balloon of omnipotence, but because he would have forced his fellow Alabamians to choose between their two heroes who didn't pussyfoot around against the Yankees.

Besides, the Bear doesn't properly belong in that line. Successful Southern politicians are pugnacious, like Wallace, perhaps mean, irascible at best. Southern generals, by contrast, are courtly and noble, permitting their troops to do the necessary bloodletting—within the rules, of course. The Bear is a general, and it is important to the state that he win his battles honorably. It is all the more significant that, during his time in the wilderness, the Bear admits to having cheated, to having wallowed in expedience; that it was only his conjoining again with Alabama that made him whole and pure once more. And what a union it has been!

There is a feeling in Alabama that most anybody can win

WINNING DESIGN By the time he was done, Bryant had chalked up more victories (323) than all coaches who came before him.

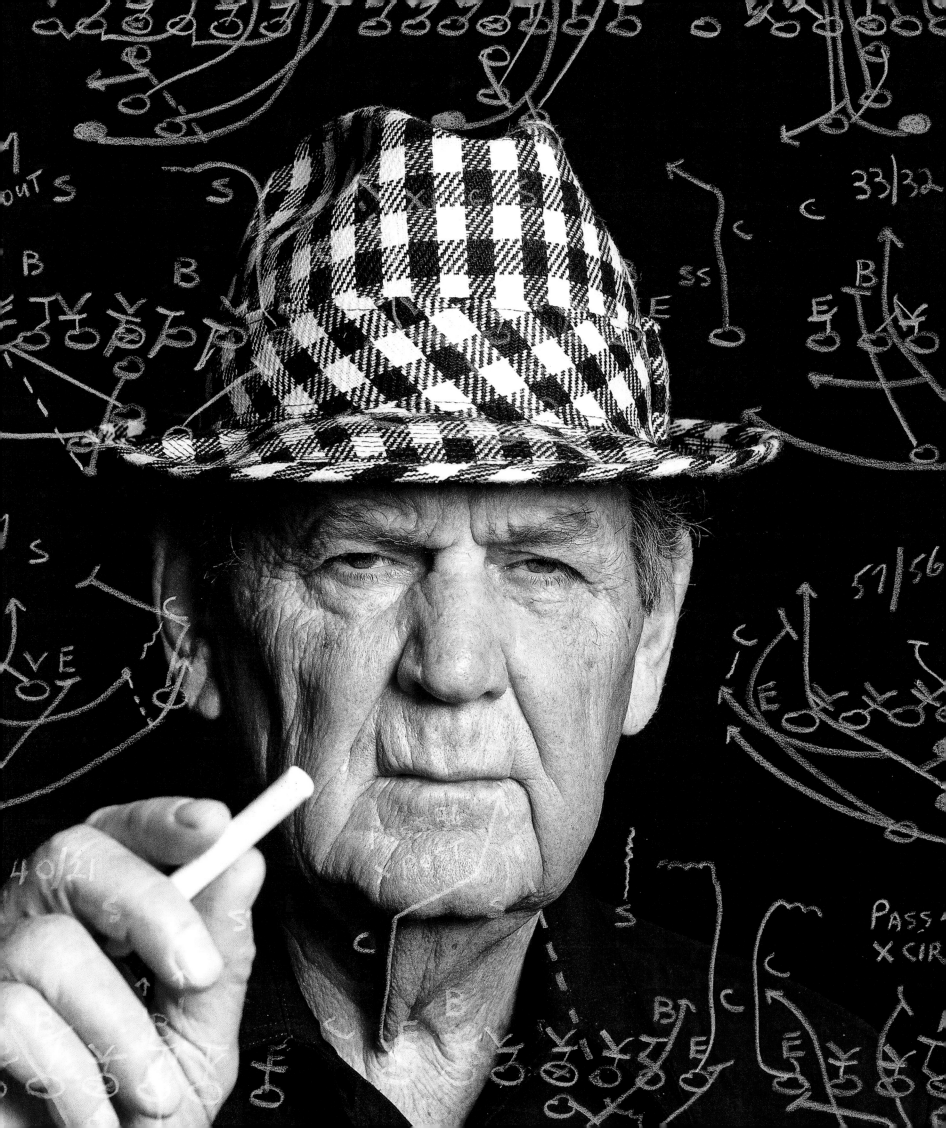

at the prominent Yankee football shelters; hell, even an old Protestant like Parseghian kept the wheel turning at Notre Dame. Larry Lacewell, the head coach at Arkansas State, who has been on the staffs at both Alabama and Oklahoma, offers this comparison: "In Oklahoma they all think they win just because it's Oklahoma. In Alabama they know why they do . . . It's him." Not even Adolph Rupp, who pretty much forced the Bear to evacuate Rupp's Kentucky fiefdom, could match him as an indigenous symbol of victory. Rupp affected the prevailing accent and became the Baron of the Bluegrass, but always and forever Kentucky knew he came from Kansas, a whole different place.

Ah, but the Bear is blood as well as guts. After musing about it for quite a while, it is only this homely theory he advances to explain why he is so especially adored in Alabama: "I'll tell you the truth. I think my playin' here had more to do with it than anything."

And, of course, the sport played was football. "Hell, used to be in the South, wasn't anything to do *but* go to a football game," the Bear says. "Well, either football or get drunk. I s'pose. Now you got more choices. Like now we got all these lakes—boats and fishin' and all that carryin' on." Understand: football isn't merely popular in the South—*football is Southern.*

Grady McWhiney and Forrest McDonald, two historians at Alabama, have advanced the theory that the Confederate temperament has been heavily influenced by the prevalence of Celts from Ireland, Scotland and Wales—and, says McDonald, "They've always been the meanest bunch of all." He goes on: "The Southerners are naturally violent, and football is the idealized ritual substitute for actual warfare. If you happen to be 10 years old, or 30, when a war breaks out, instead of being lucky enough to be 20, the Southerner—the Celt—will feel deprived of his manhood. Football can fill that void. For Alabama, the Bear is the Robert E. Lee of this warfare."

While the Bear and a winning team would have advanced the redemptive process at any time, it was, however, all the more symbolic that he happened to arrive back home at precisely the moment when the Deep South—Alabama above all—was being turned into a battlefield again. In one way or another, every white Alabamian was on the defensive, either

LESSON ONE In 1958 the new Tide coach led his first team meeting.

out of shame or to dig in: Never! But for both types there was always the Bear to celebrate, the one intrepid native who was not only succeeding, but also winning on a national scale with "skinny little white boys," as one Alabamian recalls. "There was something for everybody. Even if you weren't racist, there were certain historical imperatives to clutch to your breast. It was The War all over again; us poor, underfed, outmanned Southerners beating up on the big, ugly Yankees only because we were obviously smarter and braver."

The Bear leaves such theorizing to others. Indeed, despite once nearly being lured into politics, he remains, cannily, a man of image, not of issues. As a consequence, the Bear appears to be something of a skeleton key, a man who can unlock whatever doors—especially of the past—that his admirers want to enter. Coaching may be a young man's profession, but for the Bear, his antiquity is a real boon. Why, he's so much a part of the storied past that it's like having Lee himself around; Hank Williams, anyway.

It is certainly illuminative of his nature that the Bear took no lead whatsoever in the matter of integration. His defenders will claim that Wallace kept his hands tied, that the Bear wasn't even allowed to schedule teams with black players, much less dress any of them in crimson, and there may be a measure of truth in that. But given the Bear's surpassing popularity, he had it within his power to assume a burden of leadership. Yet he held back on race and let other—and less entrenched—Southern coaches stick their necks out first. Only after Southern Cal and Sam (Bam) Cunningham ran all over the skinny little white boys in a 1970 game, only when it was evident that the Tide couldn't win any longer lily-white, only then did the Bear learn his civics. It is consistent that the one knock against him as a coach is that he has never had the faith or the daring to be an innovator.

After all, "adjusting well" doesn't mean having to be in the vanguard. And the Bear realizes his state is naturally insular and standpat; even George Wallace, remember, for all his fulminating, was primarily a counterpuncher. Alabama still styles itself as the "Heart of Dixie," and it takes a certain contrary pride in the fact that the Sunbelt and all its alien imperfections pretty much passed it by. *Heart of Sunbelt?* Barely a generation ago Birmingham was virtually the same size as

NEW HIGH Bryant got a lift from QB Jack Hurlbut (11) and guards Bob Pettee (62) and Jimmy Sharpe (61) after topping Auburn for his first title, in 1961.

Atlanta, but now it isn't even half so populous. On campus in Tuscaloosa there is always the facetious student cry: "Thank God for Mississippi." Whatever Alabama might stand 49th in, Mississippi is sure to be 50th.

One lifelong Alabamian, a lawyer, says, chuckling sort of, "Essentially, we are sustained by the belief that we are purer than everybody but Mississippi, but better off than they are."

This backwater self-consciousness does create a sensitivity in a few of the more enlightened precincts in the Mind of Dixie, an apprehension that the more successful the Bear's football team is, the more the rather undistinguished state university, which incidentally shares its name, must suffer by comparison. The school's new president, an Alabamian and a Harvard man, Joab Thomas, has, for instance, confessed to friends how disturbed he is that the major faculty concern expressed to him so far is that their Tide tickets aren't so good as in autumns past. Indeed, for many in Tuscaloosa, the Bear's gridiron preeminence stands out as a guidon to follow into their own battles. Says Arthur Thompson, a respected professor of economics, "I see the Bear as an incentive to make all of us here ask why can't we have as much success in our areas of the university as he does in his."

Yet, as a law professor points out, one clear legacy of Wallace that lingers in the state is an intellectual perversity, a tendency to sneer at all those pointy-headed liberal wimps. In this respect, it is significant that coach Paul (Bear) Bryant is not merely indigenous and cultural, Southern and country football. He's the only game in town.

Alabama is part of that last swath of genuine football territory that hasn't been encroached upon by the pros: from the Georgia line, west through northern Louisiana and Arkansas, north including all of Tennessee, is a duchy of perhaps 15 million people, virgin to the NFL. College alumni are only a small portion of the whole fandom, which tends to think of the University of Alabama as a football team and nothing else.

Understand, if the university is a football factory, that isn't the Bear's fault. He isn't to blame that the woebegone library languishes, that professors in the English department didn't have telephones until seven months ago. Football runs deep. The most famous of President Thomas's predecessors was President George Denny, who directed funds to the construction of a stadium while having seniors teach freshmen. It was under Denny that a football recruit named Bryant was brought in, then given two courses at Tuscaloosa High to prop up his admission. Denny had seen the value of football: Alabama's Rose Bowl juggernauts had put the state on the map when precious else but the Ku Klux Klan was achieving that. Finally they named the president's greatest achievement after him: Denny Stadium. Two years ago it was renamed: Bryant–Denny Stadium.

The issue isn't simply: Does football diminish education? There are a lot of places besides Tuscaloosa where it is more popular to install AstroTurf than bookshelves. In fact a great deal of it is just that the Bear makes a game so respectable, perhaps even too much so. Surely it is revealing how many of the Tide fans dress—overdress—for the games. To kill. To the nines. The large numbers of preppie fashion plates in an Alabama football crowd make it look like something out of O'Hara rather than Faulkner. It's just another way to dress up the game, too, make it more legitimate.

By now the Bear and football in Alabama are one and the same. He is football incarnate, which will make it very difficult whenever he must depart. Oh, sure, whoever succeeds him might well keep the victories coming, might keep filling the stadiums (the Tide has a spare in Birmingham) and traveling to the bowls. But it will never be so fine again. The Bear is exalted and he, in return, makes it possible for the people in Alabama to take football more to heart than others can. So when the Bear goes, it will not just be that one more link to the past will be broken, that a little more of that curious Southern combination of eternal knighthood and childhood will fade. It will be harder for football ever to mean so much again in Alabama. Not even winning will be quite the same.

AS THE WINS HAVE PILED UP, THE Bear has become proportionately more self-effacing, exchanging his houndstooth hat for a hair shirt after every game. When the Tide wins, it is because of the assistants and the boys and their mommas and daddies, everybody but him. When Alabama loses, he marches right in to see the winning coach and starts with the *mea culpas*. Of course, this isn't all that heart-wrenching for the Bear because he knows nobody believes him anyhow. It's like the Jack Benny cheapskate routine.

Hear, for example, from Kim Norris, senior majorette—Crimsonette—who has spent all her life ("I can barely remember Joe Namath") around Tuscaloosa: "It's really depressing when it does happen, when we do lose. I just try to put it out of my mind. I mean, nobody's supposed to beat Alabama. Nobody's supposed to beat Bear Bryant. But we know it's not his fault, whatever he says. It's the quarterback who fumbled or the sun got in somebody's eyes or it's just a bad day, but it's never coach Bryant."

Probably to make it harder for anybody else to get a big head, the Bear goes on taking all the blame. Watching films of this season's Ole Miss game for the first time, he noted, after one good ground-gainer, something called the "whoopee pass": "That's the only play I called all day." Minutes later, though, on his statewide TV show, the—not surprisingly—top-rated college football program in the country, he took no credit for the whoopee pass, but when Alabama failed on

CRIMSON PRIDE Bryant, shown here before a 1970 game, was revered as a good ol' boy who took on the nation and whipped it.

fourth-and-two, he was quick to shoulder the blame. "I send in all the bad plays," he announced, shifting comfortably in his sackcloth and ashes.

Or, for variety, sometimes the Bear prefers to go the other way, which is that he doesn't coach at all, hasn't for years. "I think I was a good coach once," he says pitiably. "Now I just have good people to coach for me. I do still know a whole lot about coachin' people." Of course, in this dumb-as-a-fox routine there is a kernel of truth: However inspirational football coaches are supposed to be, however creative, the prime requisite may well be an executive ability—selecting capable lieutenants, pointing them in the right direction and then just checking the compass now and again.

There was a wonderful moment in this year's Ole Miss game when the Tide was on defense and the Bear decided he would come over and palaver with his quarterbacks. Only it turned out that all the quarterbacks were clustered around Mal Moore, the offensive coordinator, who was drawing plays on a portable blackboard set up behind the bench. And when the Bear came up from behind, he could hardly see in. Worse than that, none of the quarterbacks even knew he was there, because they were staring so intently at the blackboard. The Bear looked so foolish, sort of like a little boy trying to peer over the big folks in front to see

CUT-DOWN DAY The Bear visits the barber.

the parade going by. He would step this way and that, but he couldn't get in; there were always helmets and shoulder pads blocking his view. But did the Bear ever say word one? He did not. All he had to do was mumble boo and those shoulder pads would have parted like the Red Sea. But it was good enough for the Bear to see that the quarterbacks were all paying such strict attention to Moore—that's the whole idea, isn't it?—so, after a time, without anybody even knowing he'd been there, he just ambled off. It was a few minutes later, mulling things over, that he called the old whoopee pass.

Bum Phillips, the head coach of the New Orleans Saints, recalls the first day he worked as an assistant to the Bear, at Texas A&M: "He told me to go organize the quarterbacks and centers. I got there early, and I looked around and there weren't any footballs. I waited and waited: still, no footballs. So I walked up to coach Bryant and asked, 'You reckon those managers are gonna get those balls down here?'

"And he looked at me and said, 'Well, I don't know. But I'll tell you one damn thing. I ain't gonna get 'em.'

"On the way to gettin' the balls, I figured out the difference between the head coach and the assistant coach."

Unfortunately, a number of the 44 of the Bear's protégés who have ascended to head coaching positions have never figured that out. "The trouble is," Phillips says, "a lot of these people might have known football, but they tried to coach like they thought Bryant coached. But he doesn't coach the way they thought he coached. Why, he'd give out the impression that he'd never let a player get away with anything. But at the same time, he did. And the people who worked for him didn't even know it. And he'd make everybody think he thought they were the best on the staff. It was the same way with the players. I don't know as he ever planned a damn thing he did. He just does it."

Yet except perhaps for laying on the old-dumb-me stuff a little thick, the Bear isn't a conniving man; as much as with any celebrity, the public figure matches his private man. He truly is genuine in how he cares for his players as whole people, and not just as split ends and centers. The woods are full of old associates he came to help in their times of travail. "I'll tell you the truth," the Bear says, "I can't even go to these conventions anymore. It takes me an hour to get to an elevator, from all these 50-year-old assistants asking me to he'p 'em find a job. It just breaks my heart." He cries when an old friend dies, and he harks back to memories of Mama regularly. At home, he does what Mary Harmon tells him to do, and he still says she's the prettiest girl in the world. He raises hell with the boys, pays deference to the ladies and pats little children on the head.

In the main, in public, he has been picked dry by now. What more can be revealed about an old country fellow who has coached football all his life? But, of course, in the countdown to 315, Bearologists have multiplied. There is even a book out now, written by some modern-day Parson Weems, entitled *Young Bear: The Legend of Bear Bryant's Boyhood.* "According to the best research available, the following events in Bear Bryant's boyhood actually occurred," it says. Presumably the best research would be to ask the Bear. He's still alive. Billy Varner is still driving him all around in the Buick. But, any-

HANDING OFF Bryant's executive abilities showed in his cultivation of skilled assistants, dozens of whom went on to become head coaches.

way, here is a certified highlight of his legendary childhood:

"Paul was still 11 when he took his now famous cat to church and not long after that when he took that now famous turtle to school."

In other words, when his cats and turtles have grown "now famous," we have heard it all.

Oh, sure, people who don't know him well like to say there is a coach Paul (Bear) Bryant nobody really knows except possibly Mary Harmon and a couple of his good business pals who have made him lots of money. But who would believe a fool thing like that? If there has been another Bear hiding in the weeds all these years, then that certainly devalues the one we have gotten to know so well. "Why, you have to be yourself," the Bear says. "Least of all you can't fool players. Ain't that so, Billy?"

In fact, the only time the Bear has come a cropper has been when he stopped being himself—as in the late '60s, when all hell was breaking loose around the country.

"I just didn't know how to handle the change, so I started to think we must be winnin' by outcoachin', and anytime you think that, that's when you will get your ass whipped," he says. "Why, before that, I ate with my quarterback every day, but I got outta that, and then along came that rebellious era; that dope era, that why-you-want-me-to-do-this era. The players wanted to be like every other student, and you can't be that way and win. You just can't.

"But the biggest thing was, I was just doin' a lousy job. So when I understood that, I read the riot act to them and got back to work myself. I changed my approach too. I used to tell a player comin' in, now you're gonna have to be a little bit better player each day, and you're gonna have to do better in your academics and learn lessons every day. And if you do this, you'll be a better person and be able to take your place in society better than when you came here.

"But the kids changed, so now I start the other way, at the other end of the barrel. I tell a boy, if you're *not* a special kind of person when you come here, I don't want you. See how I turned it around? 'Course, I do still tell 'em if I can't love you and pat you and brag on you, I don't want you. I think I can do that better'n anybody."

What, exactly? Do you mean, inspire?

"I don't know. And if I did, I wouldn't tell you."

This season, as the Bear feared, as Alabama's relatively modest record attests—relative to other Crimson Tide teams, understand—he has been bedeviled by the pressures of the approaching record. At times he has betrayed his instincts and not pushed the Tide as vigorously as he believed he should for fear critics would accuse him of being selfish. It irks him, too, that the hullabaloo is somewhat manufactured.

"All I know is, I don't want to stop coaching and I don't want to stop winning, so we're gonna break the record unless I die," he says. State law will permit him to hold his job through the 1983 season, when he turns 70, but should he desire, he will almost surely stay on after that, either with an age exemption provided by special state legislation, or through an obscure NCAA provision that permits one volunteer coach per athletic department. Normally, this is somebody who comes in to handle the kayaking team or ladies' handball, but it is just as applicable to the head football coach. The Bear is wealthy enough and could keep making a pile on side deals, so coaching on the cuff would be no great hardship. In any event, whatever the arrangements to keep him in his tower, it is understood that he has delegated a couple of his closest friends to tell him the truth if he ever starts to lose his marbles. He doesn't, says a confidant, "want to pull a Rupp and have to get dragged out of here."

For now, though, there is no escaping the Hank Aaron or Pete Rose role he must play, by the numbers. Some alumni have donated a huge trailer, which is hauled back and forth between the two Tide stadiums in Tuscaloosa and Birmingham so that the Bear can address the world in style after each home game. The trailer looks rather like something a TV preacher might take on the road, with a choir. There are chairs for more than 100 press, who peer up toward where the Bear sits in something of a pulpit-type arrangement. There is a red carpet on the floor, and a clapboard wall behind him and a $4,800 sound mixer to snare and amplify his mumbled responses.

Of course, the Bear has for long been the center of a real cottage industry in Alabama, with all sorts of icons and other coach Paul (Bear) Bryant collectibles being turned out. The approaching record has served as an excuse to manufacture a whole new generation of Bear keepsakes, all "315" models: cushions, calendars, bumper stickers, banners, buttons, kerchiefs, statues and those large foam hands with the index finger raised. For folks with more expensive tastes, there are busts, guaranteed to be of a "stonelike material," at $50, commemorative coins (peaking at $1,250 for a platinum job) and paintings and original sculpture up to $4,500.

The Bear himself doesn't altogether discourage this harmless idolatry. He even turned a dollar or two once himself, in partnership with Sonny Werblin of Madison Square Garden, peddling replicas of his houndstooth hats. For the more reflective there is on display in two adjoining rooms of the Memorial Coliseum, the Coach Paul (Bear) Bryant memorabilia collection. The relics have been donated by the subject himself, and it is a solemn tribute, nearly hallowed.

Everything conceivable relating to the Bear has been exhibited: declarations, magazine covers, trophies, cartoons, keys to the city—from Sylacauga, Anniston, Florence, Gadsden and any number of other places; that is a whole section just by itself, keys to the city. There is an autographed photograph of Esther Williams.

FASHION STATEMENT Bryant's signature houndstooth hat is one of the most memorable accessories in the history of sport.

And every picture of the Bear identifies him as *Coach* Bryant. It isn't only Coach Bryant and Lana Turner and Coach Bryant and Joe DiMaggio, it's Coach Bryant and Herman Hickman, Coach Bryant and Ara Parseghian, Coach Bryant and Bud Wilkinson. There is only the one coach.

NOW ON THIS PARTICULAR sweltering day in the middle of last summer, the memorabilia rooms were almost asphyxiating people because the rooms had been shut up since school let out. The only reason they had been opened was because Frank House, the old catcher with the Detroit Tigers, had come down from Birmingham. House is a well-spoken man in his 50s, trim and handsome, but he has always been known as Pig around home—Pig House. He was in the rooms with Charley Thornton, an assistant athletic director, because the Bear had given Pig permission to take some of the objects for the Alabama Sports Hall of Fame.

All of a sudden, here comes the Bear himself, wet from the heat, shuffling along, looking exceptionally old, his seersucker pants drooping down. He acted as if he had just stumbled this way, even though it was far down at the other end of the coliseum, on another floor, from his air-conditioned offices, and Billy was waiting to take him home to Mary Harmon. Obviously, someone had told him, Hey, Coach, you know Pig House is down there taking things out of your memorabilia rooms.

House looked up in distress; Thornton came to his aid. "You remember, Coach," he said quickly, "you told Pig he could take some of your stuff up to the Hall of Fame."

"Sure I remember," the Bear replied. "I just want to see *what* it is he's takin', that's all." And he came into the sweatbox and started examining all the things about coach Bryant. It was like Huck Finn attending his own funeral.

Pig reported about which of the items he had already put in his Cadillac. "O.K.," the Bear said, and he started searching the walls himself. He already looked a whole lot younger than when he had stepped into the place. He didn't even look

LONGTIME LOVE Bryant and Mary Harmon married in 1935.

as hot anymore. "Here!" he called out. "SEC coach, alltime. Now that's not a bad thing, either. Alltime SEC coach."

House and Thornton couldn't agree more, and hurried to get the SEC citation off the wall. "And Coach of the Decade. National. Where's that?" the Bear asked. "Let's find that one." The three of them started searching for that award, too, but it just couldn't be located anywhere. You just cannot believe how much stuff is jammed into those memorabilia rooms.

At last, Thornton tried to help out. "How 'bout this, sir? The Arkansas Hall of Fame certificate?"

Look out. That was the wrong thing to say.

"No, sir!" the Bear thundered. He wasn't mumbling any now. "Why it took them five years to put Hutson in, and he was a better player than anybody else even *walked* across Arkansas. They asked me to speak that year, and I flat wouldn't do it. No, sir. Then it took 'em another 10 years 'fore they put me in. They had *girls* and ever'thin' else in 'fore me. *No . . .sir!*"

So much for the Arkansas Hall of Fame. They all went back to searching for Coach of the Decade. "Wait, I got one," the Bear suddenly cried. "The Kentucky Man of the Year. Why, you know what? I got that when Alben Barkley, who was from Kentucky, was the Vice President of the United States."

So everybody abandoned the Coach of the Decade hunt and got into looking for the Kentucky Man of the Year.

And just for an instant there, glancing about, the Bear found himself face-to-face with an old picture of himself—young and strong and handsome, curly-haired and clear-eyed, and he didn't know anybody was watching, and he couldn't help but peer at himself. Hell, he sees his countenance all the time. It's on just about every product in the Heart of Dixie. But this was different. Old coach Bryant just couldn't help but share a moment with young coach Bryant.

And a smile creased his lips. Still being a coach at 68, still being coach Paul (Bear) Bryant is better even than being a legend in your own time. In a couple more weeks, two-a-days would be starting again, and the world would be young once more, and Alabama true. ❧

LAST MILE Bryant announced his retirement as Alabama coach on Dec. 15, 1982; he died a little more than a month later, on Jan. 26, 1983, at age 69.

Iron Bowl
ULTIMATE

1961 | THE AUBURN-ALABAMA feud embroils fans so deeply that the outcome of the game can define a season. The Tide won this one 34–0.

RIVALRY

BY MARK BECHTEL

PHOTOGRAPH BY MARVIN E. NEWMAN

Mark Bechtel, who moved to Alabama at age nine, recalls how he learned very quickly that the annual Auburn-Alabama game is like no other. —from SI, AUGUST 30, 2006

PERHAPS THE MOST STRIKING thing one notices upon spending one's first Iron Bowl Day in the state of Alabama is how there's no one on the streets. This works out very well, as my mom discovered, if you want to go grocery shopping. With everyone huddled up in front of a TV, decked out in crimson or orange and blue—or, if they're lucky, at the game, decked out in crimson or orange and blue—the good parking spots are yours, and you're not going to be jostling with anyone over the freshest tomatoes.

When we moved to Huntsville six weeks before the 1980 Iron Bowl, we weren't strangers to the idea of people being insane about football. We moved from Cleveland, which had its share of folks who got a little too worked up on Sunday afternoons. (My parents were Browns season-ticket holders for years.) Sure, we'd heard the stories about how big college football was in Alabama. But nothing really prepares you for what you see: the ubiquitous T-shirts, the bumper stickers, the flags flying outside homes and the oil paintings on living room walls inside them.

It's a cliché to say that football is a way of life in Alabama, but that's why someone went to the trouble of inventing clichés. At no time is the import placed on the sport more evident than in late November. As host of the state's most-listened-to sports radio show, Paul Finebaum has spent much of the last decade moderating talks on the Iron Bowl, so forgive him if he waxes hyperbolic. "In a way they wage war 365 days a year," he told me a few years ago. "It never stops, no matter who tries to intervene or referee."

No, there's no third party in the mix. There are two clearly defined sides, which was a departure from what I was used to in Cleveland, where everyone is a Browns fan. You live in Cleveland, you hate the Steelers. And if you want to take that up with a Steelers fan, you've got to drive to Pennsylvania. In Alabama, though, if you want to meet the enemy, you've only

got to walk outside. It's a sensitive environment, as I learned shortly after moving. Someone—an Auburn fan, no doubt—told me a joke involving Bear Bryant, a pig and a punch line that disparaged the coach's appearance. I told it to a 'Bama fan. It didn't go over well.

I should have learned a lesson from the glares I received (thankfully, that's all I received), namely that you can't play both sides of the fence. But that didn't stop me from having dalliances with both schools, the approximate equivalent of showing up at the Battle of Bull Run in gray pants and a blue coat. Shortly after we moved, my parents got me a 'Bama cowboy hat, for reasons known only to them, which presumably marked me as a Crimson Tide fan. Not long after the pig joke incident, I was decked out in an Auburn jersey. That didn't last either.

What I was slowly learning with all of these not-so-bitter breakups was that allegiances in Alabama are ingrained. 'Bama fans are hardwired to be 'Bama fans. (Ditto for Auburn fans.) There is no choice, and no "learning to love" a team. I recall an instance in sixth grade in which we had to bring in our most cherished possession and talk about it in front of the class; one kid, who had never before taken an assignment seriously, gave a remarkably touching account of his affection for a copy of SPORTS ILLUSTRATED with Bear Bryant on the cover. I knew I'd never be able to do that—and that I'd never fully fit in.

I wasn't the only outsider to whom this dedication was a foreign concept. Bill Curry grew up in Atlanta, played and later coached at Georgia Tech and had a 10-year career as an NFL center. In 1987 he was hired to coach the Crimson Tide. "I played in three Super Bowls—heated national, international stories—so I felt like I was a man of the world," Curry told me. "When I got to Alabama, people said, 'You don't understand how this is going to be with Alabama and Auburn.' I said, 'Don't worry. I understand intense football.'" Here Curry paused. "I did not have a clue."

In time he realized that the sport is so important because it has long been a source of state pride, something that was not easy to come by in the 1950s and '60s. "You had Bull Connor, church bombings, the hoses, the dogs, the nightmare of all that," said Curry. "Southerners were embarrassed—as well we should have been. The one thing that wasn't embarrassing was

COACH SPEAK The Tigers' Shug Jordan chatted up the Bear in 1970.

MEETING HALFWAY Before 1989, when it became a home-and-home series, the Iron Bowl was played at neutral Legion Field in Birmingham.

when Bear and his little old skinny boys whipped up on other football teams, especially the Yankee football teams."

But there's more to it than whipping a bunch of Yankees. It's much more fun to whip the guy down the street, to see the hurt on his face after the game—and every day for the next 364. That's what makes the Alabama-Auburn game what it is. It defines a season. In 1987 Curry's team lost to Auburn 10–0. In '88 his club won nine games but lost to Auburn 15–10. The next summer he was stopped by an elderly woman on campus. "She was pained in her expression and had tears in her eyes," he recalled. "She reached up and took my arms in her hands, and all she said was, 'Coach, do you think we can win this year?' And I knew exactly what she meant." In '89 Curry took a 10–0 team that was ranked No. 2 in the country down to Auburn and lost 30–20.

In 1990 Curry was coaching at Kentucky.

Bear's record-setter

The upshot is, as detestable as Crimson Tide fans find Tigers backers (and vice versa), they need each other. Auburn is the yin to Alabama's yang. They complete each other. Without the Iron Bowl, college football in Alabama is no different from college football in Nebraska or Georgia or anywhere else where one school is king. But with the Iron Bowl, that boast on the facade of the upper deck at Legion Field—FOOTBALL CAPITAL OF THE SOUTH—becomes an unnecessarily modest statement. Alabama is the college football capital of the world.

ON THE FIRST SATURDAY MORNING in December 1948, the student-body presidents of Alabama and Auburn dug a hole in Woodrow Wilson Park in downtown Birmingham. Then they dropped a hatchet into the hole and covered it with dirt. With the hatchet symbolically buried—and safely out of the hands of their schools' sometimes crazed fans—they went off to watch their football teams square off for the first time in four decades. "There were a lot of hard feelings between the students," Gillis Cammack, the Auburn student-body president in '48, told me three years ago. "We were trying to get everyone to settle down and not be so vicious."

Though the football teams hadn't met since a 1907 dispute between Auburn and Alabama over petty matters that included how many players could travel to the game and where the officials would come from, the fierceness of the rivalry had not diminished. The war of words has never let up. 'Bama fans have been calling it *Aubarn* since the school on the Plains, originally a private college, was given to the state in 1872 for use as a land-grant institution. Bear Bryant referred to his archrival simply as "that cow college." Dennis Franchione,

RUNAWAY VICTORY Johnny Musso led the Tide's charge in 1971.

who coached the Tide in 2001 and '02, seldom uttered the name of the university 165 miles southeast of Tuscaloosa. "That school down the road," he called it.

Fearing that fans might brawl when the series resumed in '48, Bull Connor, the Birmingham police chief who 15 years later would gain national infamy for attacking peaceful civil rights protesters in his city with police dogs and fire hoses, called Cammack and a few other students into his office the week before the game and warned them that he would not tolerate any trouble. He got none, as 43,954 fans packed Legion Field—which would serve as the game's neutral site for the next 40 years—and politely watched the Crimson Tide destroy the Tigers 55–0. The next year Auburn exacted revenge, winning 14–13.

Elephant stomp

Since then the series has provided a host of memorable moments. Ken Stabler's Run in the Mud in 1967. Bear Bryant's record 315th win in 1981. Van Tiffin's 52-yard field goal in the dying seconds in '85. Sam Shade and Tommy Johnson's fourth-down tackle in 1994, preserving a 'Bama win. Not all of the memories are so fond for Tide fans, though. In 1972 Bear's boys were undefeated and ranked No. 2 in the country. They held a 16–3 lead over the Tigers in the fourth quarter, but Auburn's Bill Newton blocked two punts, and David Langner returned both for touchdowns, as the Tigers rallied for a 17–16 win. The Tide's national title hopes were shot, and Auburn had fodder for a sticker that can still be seen on some of its fans' bumpers: PUNT, BAMA, PUNT. Shortly after moving to the state, Finebaum spent Thanksgiving with a family whose postfeast tradition was to retire to the parlor to listen to a phonograph recording of that game.

The level of passion has never varied, but the rivalry itself has undergone some changes. Sick of going to Birmingham every year, Auburn insisted on playing every other game in Jordan-Hare Stadium, starting in 1989. In 2000 Alabama moved its home games in the series to Tuscaloosa, so now the crowds are partisan. "It was really something special when it was played in Birmingham and the fans were split 50-50," Curry said. "The intensity never relented because half the stadium had something to cheer for all the time."

I talked to Cammack 55 years after he dug that hole in Woodrow Wilson Park, and there was an Alabama-Auburn game fast approaching. He was 79, but he vowed he'd be watching the game from his home in Selma. Then I asked about the hatchet. He had no idea what had become of it. Woodrow Wilson Park has undergone several renovations—it is now called Linn Park—and there is nothing to mark the burial site, which probably doesn't matter anyway. Said Cammack, "I doubt if that hatchet stayed buried very long." ∽

STOP SIGN Auburn's James Bostic and his team were shut out in 1992.

GALLERY OF GREATS

PHOTOGRAPH BY JAMES DRAKE

KENNY STABLER *Quarterback* 1965–67

Bear Bryant once said of the young Snake, "You can never tell about lefthanded quarterbacks and lefthanded crapshooters." In the end Stabler's record left little room for doubt. The Tide went 28-3-2 in his three years, and as a starter in 1966 he led Alabama to an 11–0 record and was named Orange Bowl MVP.

DON HUTSON

WIDE RECEIVER 1932–34

Decades after he left the University of Alabama, the wideout who revolutionized his position remained a storied figure around the Tuscaloosa campus.

—*excerpted from* SI, SEPTEMBER 20, 1965

BOTH BEFORE, DURING AND after Don Hutson caught all of those passes in 1934, the stars fell regularly on Alabama. Ahead of Hutson were, for example, Johnny Mack Brown, Hoyt Winslett, Fred Sington and Johnny Cain. With him were Dixie Howell, who threw the passes, and Riley Smith and—alas—the *other* end, Bear Bryant. And then after him came Joe Kilgrow, Jimmy Nelson, Harry Gilmer, Bart Starr, Lee Roy Jordan and Joe Namath. Alabama has produced 28 All-America football players and turned out seven undefeated teams in the last 41 years (six of them posting the best record in the nation). Only Notre Dame has enjoyed a more illustrious football history. Despite all this fast company, however, Alabama today derives most of its sustaining spirit from Hutson, the Pine Bluff, Ark., youth who brought speed, moves and hands to the delicate art of catching passes.

It is quite possible that Hutson was the finest receiver football has ever known. The Green Bay Packers, for whom he made so many spectacular plays in his professional career after leaving Alabama, would not disagree, nor would any of the National Football League's defensive backs who tried to cover him. Hutson caught passes while speeding into the clear, in "traffic," as the saying goes, with one hand—either one. He caught them diving, falling, lying down, jumping, bending, swinging around a goalpost, and stealing them out of others' hands. He not only made the catches, he ran like a thief thereafter, for this was a superb athlete who could have excelled at baseball, basketball or track if he had not chosen football.

HIS STYLE CAUGHT ON

Foremost among the Hutson stories that are still told on the campus at Tuscaloosa is the one concerning his love for other games. Once during an Alabama baseball game Hutson wore his track suit underneath his flannels—it's really true—because a dual meet was scheduled simultaneously on the track adjacent to the diamond. Between innings, he stripped off the baseball uniform, got into the starting blocks and ran a 9.8 100-yard dash!

That is the big thing some people forget about Hutson—the speed that propelled him beyond his defenders and enabled him to catch 488 passes for the Packers, scoring 101 touchdowns in the NFL in 11 seasons, setting so many records that only now, 21 years since he retired, are today's stars catching up with him.

"The thing you remember best about him is how calm and relaxed he always was," says Bear Bryant. "He could go to sleep on the bench before the Rose Bowl game." And then, as he did, catch five of six passes from Howell for 123 yards, another for a 54-yard touchdown from substitute quarterback Joe Riley, helping to destroy Stanford 29–13 and giving the 1934 Alabama team a perfect 10–0 record for the season.

Recruiting is as old as football itself, and Hutson, after being spotted catching five touchdown passes in a single game for Pine Bluff, was one of eight Arkansas athletes shepherded to Tuscaloosa in 1931 and '32—some of the others being Bryant and J.B. (Ears) Whitworth, Charlie Marr and Rip Hewes. It was not until his senior year, however, that Hutson became the incomparable receiver who fascinated the whole collegiate world. As coach Frank Thomas's team steadily defeated its opponents, Hutson got better and more sensational, not only catching but running blazing end-around plays.

Yet even as he looks back on his career today, Hutson—now the owner of a well-established automobile business in Racine, Wis.—is modest. "Dixie Howell was a great college passer," says he. "I always knew if I ran like the devil, the ball would be there."

FIRST-CLASS PLAYER When the college and pro halls of fame began admitting inductees, each tabbed Hutson as one of their charter members.

BETTMANN/CORBIS (JORDAN); DAMIAN STROHMEYER (THOMAS)

LEE ROY JORDAN *Linebacker* 1960–62

Heading into the 1963 Orange Bowl against Oklahoma, Jordan's defense had not allowed more than a touchdown in 24 straight games. Oklahoma was still favored in that game, but the senior captain made sure that Alabama ruled the day. The All-America made an astounding 31 tackles in a 17–0 win.

DERRICK THOMAS *Linebacker* 1985–88

His position coach, Sylvester Croom, compared Thomas's rush to a basketball player's crossover dribble for the way he had opponents hurtling in the wrong direction. Those moves sure worked: Thomas established a school record with 18 sacks in '87 and then topped that mark with 27 in '88, which earned him the Butkus Award.

ERIC CURRY *Defensive End* 1990–92

The speedy All-America, in tandem with end John Copeland, brought the backfield pressure for a dominating defense that helped Alabama finish the 1992 season undefeated and capture the school's first national championship of the post–Bear Bryant era.

CHRIS SAMUELS *Offensive Tackle* 1996–99

He stood 6' 6" and weighed 291 pounds, but what was really impressive about the Outland Trophy winner was his speed. "Chris is so agile, you'd swear he weighs 250," Alabama offensive coordinator Neil Callaway told SI before the 1999 season. "He's the best lineman I've ever been around."

NEIL LEIFER

JOE NAMATH

QUARTERBACK 1962-64

In the special college football issue that surveyed the nation's best quarterbacks, Alabama's brash import from Pennsylvania was given a closer look. —*excerpted from* SI, SEPTEMBER 23, 1963

ALABAMA ALREADY HAD Auburn convinced. The score was 38–0 with two minutes to play in Birmingham, and all that remained undone in the season was for sophomore quarterback Joe Namath to secure the 37 yards he needed to break Alabama's alltime total-offense record set by Harry Gilmer in 1945. It was third down and 13 on the Alabama 28, and one pass would get it all. Namath huddled with his team and then gave the order. Alabama quick-kicked.

Naturally, after that, Namath could not break Gilmer's record. Naturally, too, Bear Bryant admired him, not just for his selflessness but also for the guts it takes to play the defensive game that Bryant espouses. These qualities help make Namath the second-best—to George Mira—quarterback in the South.

To be sure, Namath knows offense too. He passed and rushed for 1,421 yards, and 13 of his 76 completed passes went for touchdowns last year. This spring the normally noncommittal Bryant dared to say, "I will be disappointed if Joe Namath is not the greatest quarterback in the South—ever. I will also be greatly disappointed if he is not the best quarterback in the country."

What Namath already is is the only Yankee on the Alabama team. He came to Tuscaloosa from Beaver Falls, Pa., for two unshakable reasons: He "wanted to play football in the South," and he wanted to play football for Bear Bryant. Known in high school as the Hungarian Howitzer, he had offers of football scholarships from 52 colleges, and a Chicago Cubs baseball scout was talking in terms of a $50,000 bonus. Once in the South the talented Namath told Alabama reporters as a freshman that it was "nice" that Bryant had varsity quarterback Jack Hurlbut coming back because "I might get hurt." The following spring, true to his word, he won the starting job, and one day as he huddled with his cast of upperclassmen he piped: "Fellows, this is an option play. But I think old Joe's going to run with it. Let's see some blocking. Coach Bryant don't want to get me hurt." ♋

KEY BOOSTER Bear Bryant once referred to Namath, who led the Tide to the 1964 championship, as the greatest athlete he ever coached.

JOHN HANNAH *Guard* 1970–72

"Hannah is about the greatest thing you ever saw." That opinion was rendered by Bear Bryant to SI in 1972, when the guard was grading a path for Alabama's resurgent running game. In '81 an SI cover would declare that Hannah, then a New England Patriot, was "the best offensive lineman of all time."

OZZIE NEWSOME *Split End* 1974–77

Alternating between split end and tight end, the position he would play in the NFL, Newsome defined versatility. He was a dangerous enough deep threat to average 20.3 yards per reception for the Tide and a punishing enough blocker to be voted the SEC's lineman of the year as a senior.

MIKE MAPLE (LYONS); JIM GUND (LANGHAM)

MARTY LYONS *Defensive Tackle* 1976–78

He was the defensive captain of the 1978 championship team that shut down Penn State all Sugar Bowl long, and most memorably in a fourth-quarter goal line stand. Lyons was named an All-America in '78, and the team went 31–5 during his three seasons in Tuscaloosa.

ANTONIO LANGHAM *Defensive Back* 1990–93

A winner of the Jim Thorpe Award for the nation's top defensive back, Langham had 19 career interceptions, including one that decided the inaugural SEC championship game, in 1992: Alabama and Florida were tied late in the fourth quarter when Langham picked off a Shane Matthews pass and returned it for a touchdown.

JOHNNY MUSSO

RUNNING BACK 1969–71

Pat Putnam's "Pride in the Red Jersey" described how Musso helped Bear Bryant revive a program that had suffered several down years. —*excerpted from* SI, OCTOBER 11, 1971

FOR WHAT MUST HAVE SEEMED an eternity to the rest of the coaching profession, Paul Bryant and his little bitty Tidesmen were the executioners of the Southeastern Conference—and of anyone else unfortunate enough to get in their path. They plucked national championships as easily as other people picked grapes.

Then odd things began to happen to the University of Alabama. For one, two-platoon football caught up with Bryant's small linemen. The Goliaths were getting a chance to rest so that when they did play, they not only came in big but also fast. The Bear's passing attack began to fire blanks. The superb defenses began to give up points in bunches of 41 and 49 and 47, a whole season's worth in a vintage year. Losses came in clusters of fives. In 1969 even *Vanderbilt* beat Alabama. And there was the time that same year when, after Tennessee had humbled the Tide 41–14, Volunteer linebacker Steve Kiner came up to Bryant and said, "Gee, Coach, they don't seem to have the same pride in wearing that red jersey anymore." Bryant will never forget Kiner's words.

This season the pride—and the Tide—are back, as was completely apparent in Birmingham last Saturday when Alabama bit, chewed and digested previously unbeaten Mississippi 40–6.

One day last week Bryant sat in his office in Tuscaloosa and dissected what had happened. Mostly he used the scalpel on himself. "We kind of lost something the last two years," he said softly. "Confidence in ourselves . . . leadership. I blame myself. I've done a lousy job lately. I guess I got to a point where I just expected things to happen instead of making them happen. People were licking their chops to get at us. Before, well, they weren't real anxious to play us."

He stubbed out a cigarette, lit another one. For a moment he stared at the photographs of his classic teams of the early 1960s that hang on the wall opposite his desk. "We're starting to get it back now," he said. He pointed at the photos. "Confidence is what those teams had, and that's what we're rebuilding."

Bryant began reconstructing Alabama almost before anyone knew it was about to collapse. After last spring's practice Bryant made a major change. He came away convinced he could no longer succeed with the drop-back passer. "We had a good one last year in Scott Hunter, a real pro-style thrower, and we couldn't win," he said. So he junked the passing attack that until recent seasons had terrorized the SEC. "After a helluva big gut check," he said. But Bryant has never feared change.

That done, Bryant assessed his team's strengths. For openers there was Johnny Musso, a 191-pound halfback known as the Italian Stallion. "Johnny can do everything," says Bryant. "He's a great runner, blocker and passer. If we let him, he'd be a great defensive back too. Last year he had to run his own interference and he still gained over 1,100 yards. The ideal situation would be Musso running with Musso up front blocking for him."

Late Saturday afternoon Mississippi, third in the SEC in passing and last in total defense, arrived in Birmingham, unbeaten in three starts. From the beginning the Rebels knew they were in for a rugged afternoon. On the first two drives Musso carried the ball eight times for 41 yards. "We just weren't getting the ball to him enough," Bryant said. "Of course, it's a problem. We'd rather have him carrying the ball, but at the same time we'd rather have him blocking. On our first drive against Florida, we go to their six in 12 plays and Johnny hasn't seen the ball yet."

For the game Musso ran 22 times for 193 yards, with few of them coming in the position you might expect from a runner, totally upright. Usually Musso is in the act of falling, only he never quite does. He gets hit, bounces along on one leg for a while, then spins, leans over backward and picks up another yard or two, and then for a finale puts a hand down and scrambles as far as he can before the rest of the world jumps on his back.

"I don't know which I like best," Bryant said. "Watching Musso run or watching him block. He simply wipes out people when he blocks."

Which is exactly what Alabama is doing in the old bruising Bear Bryant style: wiping people out, nose to nose, jaw to jaw. Once again there is pride in the red jersey. ꝏ

CRIMSON STALLION Musso, who made the All-America teams in 1970 and '71, rushed for 2,741 yards and scored 38 touchdowns at Alabama.

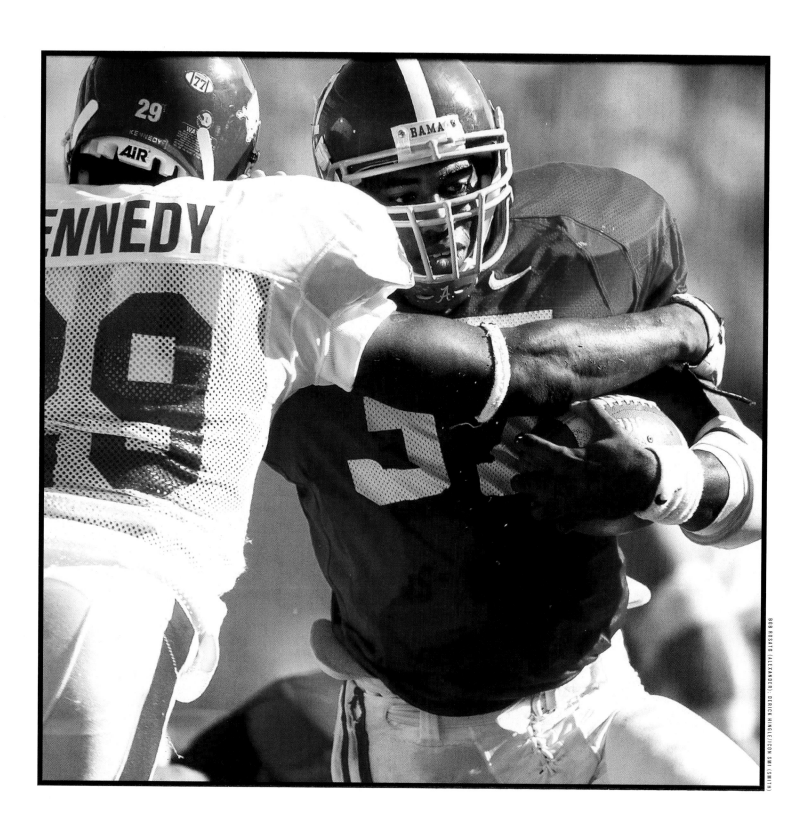

SHAUN ALEXANDER *Running Back* 1996–99

His most memorable performance may have come in the 1999 Iron Bowl, when he scored three touchdowns in the fourth quarter against Auburn to power a 28–17 come-from-behind win. But Alexander's story is one of consistent excellence: He finished his career with 15 100-yard rushing games and 50 total touchdowns.

ANDRE SMITH *Offensive Tackle* 2006–08

Nick Saban said of the 6' 4", 325-pound Smith, "It is unusual to see a guy that size who has that balance and body control. You never see him falling down, never see him off balance, and he's got a lot of power." That's how the 2008 Outland Trophy winner allowed only seven sacks over three seasons.

ROLANDO McCLAIN
Linebacker 2007–09

Teammate Javier Arenas said of the savvy McClain, "Just picture Coach Saban being huge and able to play football." In 2009 McClain joined Derrick Thomas as the only 'Bama backers to win the Butkus Award.

THE ALLTIME TEAM

OFFENSE

QB | KENNY STABLER *1965–67*

RB | SHAUN ALEXANDER *1996–99*

RB | JOHNNY MUSSO *1969–71*

RB | HARRY GILMER *1944–47*

SE | DON HUTSON *1932–34*

T | CHRIS SAMUELS *1996–99*

G | JOHN HANNAH *1970–72*

C | SYLVESTER CROOM *1972–74*

G | WAYNE FREEMAN *1962–64*

T | ANDRE SMITH *2006–08*

SE | OZZIE NEWSOME *1974–77*

DEFENSE

DE | ERIC CURRY *1990–92*

DT | MARTY LYONS *1976–78*

DT | JOHN HAND *1982–85*

DE | LEROY COOK *1972–75*

LB | DERRICK THOMAS *1985–88*

LB | LEE ROY JORDAN *1960–62*

LB | CORNELIUS BENNETT *1983–86*

LB | ROLANDO McCLAIN *2007–09*

DB | ANTONIO LANGHAM *1990–93*

DB | KEVIN JACKSON *1995–96*

DB | DON McNEAL *1977–79*

SPECIAL TEAMS

K | MICHAEL PROCTOR *1992–95*   **P** | GREG GANTT *1971–73*

KR/PR | HARRY GILMER *1944–47*

COACH

BEAR BRYANT *1958–82*

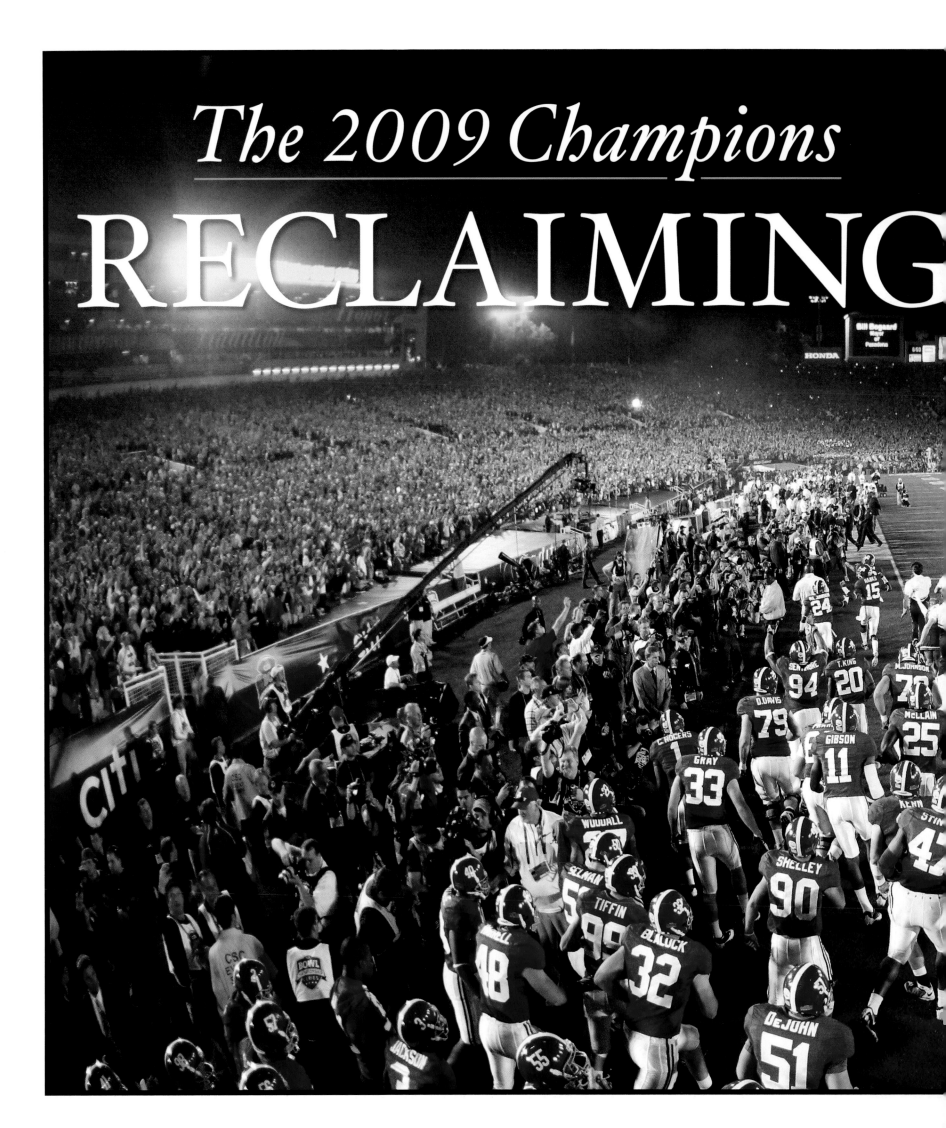

The 2009 Champions
RECLAIMING

THE CROWN

PHOTOGRAPH BY ROBERT BECK

WELCOME BACK Pasadena, the site of ancient Alabama glory, again proved to be a propitious place for the Tide to end its season.

THE CONDUCTOR Greg McElroy directed the offense on a night when his drop backs were few. | *Photograph by* ROBERT BECK

THE HIT This blow from Marcell Dareus (far right) knocked Texas quarterback Colt McCoy out of the game in the first quarter. | *Photograph by* PETER READ MILLER

THE COACH

BY RICK BRAGG

After Nick Saban was hired, how excited were fans? An April intrasquad game drew 92,000 of them. The promise of what lay ahead was in the air. —*excerpted from* SI, AUGUST 27, 2007

IT FELT GOOD. IT FELT LIKE IT USED to feel. They came from Sand Mountain, the wire grass, the Black Belt, the Gulf Coast and just wide places in the road. They came in motor homes, private jets, $30,000 pickup trucks, $400 cars and dime-store flip-flops to see Nick Saban walk the sideline of Bryant–Denny Stadium in April.

They have welcomed him as Caesar, as pharaoh, and paid him enough money to burn a wet dog. Now he will take them forward by taking them back to the glory of their past—the 21 Southeastern Conference championships, the 12 national championships, the Team of the 20th Century (as *The Wall Street Journal* called the Crimson Tide in 2000).

Saban has not promised them so much—"I don't believe in predictions," he says—but they believe. It may take two years, three, more, to be in the discussion again when people talk about the best teams in college football. But they know he will take them home.

"I've been on this roller coaster for a long time," says Ken Fowler, a 73-year-old self-made businessman who could live a lot of places but settled on a house so close to the campus that he can all but see his reflection in the go-go boots of the Crimsonettes as they strut down University Boulevard before the homecoming game. "In the '50s, under coach J.B. (Ears) Whitworth, we went 14 games without a win, and I watched grown men cry. People said then there would never be another coach here as good as Wallace Wade [who won national championships in 1925, '26 and '30] or Frank Thomas [1934, '41]. They said it was over.

"Then in '58 we hired a coach who could do the things we needed to put us in a position to win SEC championships again and national championships again. People used to stare at him as he stood on the sideline, too, like he was about to turn a stick into a snake."

His name was Paul Bryant, and he was popular here. They named an animal after him. How people loved that man. But it is time, past time, to love again.

"There is never anything wrong with remembering the past, but you can't live in it," says Mal Moore, the Alabama athletic director who was all but dragged through saw briars when it appeared that Saban and other marquee names—most notably West Virginia coach Rich Rodriguez—were passing Alabama by. Then on Jan. 3 he brought Saban home with him on the school jet from Miami, where Saban had been coaching the Dolphins. People who had been calling for Moore's resignation praised his leadership.

There is no nice way to say it: The Alabama faithful are done with waiting, with mediocrity and with disappointment, and they are finished with coaches who cannot gut out the expectations here, or who might have done well, someday, with more time or a railroad car full of luck. "We wanted a man who had won a championship, and Nick Saban is that and more," says Moore. "Saban brings a sense of command, a sense of toughness and discipline."

Saban is no rainmaker, no snake oil salesman. The way to his mountaintop is hard and paved with woe. "We can be part of something, build something all these people can be proud of and excited about again," says the 55-year-old coach, who can look intense even when he is not mad and probably looks that way holding a kitten. "I got on our guys in a team meeting. I said, 'I'm tired of hearing all this talk about a national championship when you guys don't know how to get in out of the rain, don't know what to do in the classroom.' It's like you've got little kids in the backseat, saying, 'Are we there yet?'

"The journey itself is important, not just the destination. You have to follow direction. Discipline, off-season recruiting, conditioning, practice, more recruiting, player development, classroom development. I'm not interested in what should be, could be, was. I'm interested in what is, what we control. And when we lose—and we will, one game, two, or more—we have to have a trust that what we are doing will work, trust and belief in who we are. And you get where you're going, one mile marker at a time."

Saban has yet to coach a down for the Crimson Tide, but people are already naming their children for him. Tim and Hannah Witt of Hartselle, Ala., named their baby boy, born March 20, Saban Hardin Witt. They already had a son named Tyde. "At first I thought my husband was crazy," says Hannah, "but it grew on me."

In these parts you do not name a child for a coach you expect to go 8–5. ✍

RIGHT DIRECTION With rings from LSU and now Alabama, Saban is the first coach since the AP poll began in 1936 to win national titles at two schools.

RARE AIR 'Bama relied largely on the run, but Julio Jones had an early catch that set up the Tide's first touchdown. | *Photograph by* BOB ROSATO

HAPPY RETURN Not only did defensive end Dareus intercept an ill-timed shovel pass by Garrett Gilbert just before halftime, but the sophomore then trampled over McCoy's replacement on the way to the end zone. His 28-yard return gave the Tide a 24–6 lead. | *Photographs by* ROBERT BECK *(above)*; RICHARD MACKSON *(opposite)*

JUMPING AHEAD Mark Ingram ran for two touchdowns in the game; here he edges closer to his second. | *Photograph by* ROBERT BECK

THE HEISMAN WINNER

BY SELENA ROBERTS

Before his winning the Heisman, Roberts reported on sophomore running back Mark Ingram and his relationship with his imprisoned father. —*excerpted from* SI, NOVEMBER 30, 2009

THE PRECIOUS CONNECTION between father and son is a TV cable inside a windowless warehouse turned prison. You wouldn't know that former NFL wideout Mark Ingram lives here—or that any federal inmate does, for that matter. The Queens Private Correctional Facility is unmarked, blending into an industrial district used by dozens of express shipping companies that fly cargo in and out of nearby Kennedy Airport. Ingram doesn't want to leave it. He doesn't seek transport to a permanent institution with roomy outdoor space. He doesn't itch for a facility with a stocked library. Because what would he do if he lost the remote?

In the common room at Queens, Ingram has game-day TV privileges he might not have somewhere else. He has been able to watch Little Mark, as the family calls running back Mark Ingram Jr., carry the second-ranked Alabama Crimson Tide into the national-title conversation. He has been the main cat in the Wildcat and the unshakable go-to player for an undefeated Tide team. "It's humbling to have the team believe in me," says Ingram Jr.

Mark Jr. has given 'Bama a splash of star power reminiscent of the Joe Namath and Kenny Stabler days. "And neither of them won a Heisman," reminds Taylor Watson, Tide historian and curator of the Bear Bryant museum in Tuscaloosa. "Alabama has a long list of great players, but no one has ever won it. People here walk a fine line. We like to say how we're only about winning and not Heisman trophies, but that talk might be different if Alabama had one."

When Little Mark was truly little, Big Mark would wear a ball cap twisted backward in a trendy, if strained, effort to keep up with youth when he helped coach the high school track team at Southwestern Academy in Flint, Mich., in the spring of 2008. Some days, as he crouched into the starters' blocks, he would shake his legs in the donkey-kick action sprinters use to loosen up their limbs. "I'm an old man, but I can still beat you," he would tell Little Mark, then a senior. Ingram's face had become rounder and his body softer since his NFL days ended in 1996, but he maintained that quick first step of a poked cat. Little Mark was a low-slung version of his dad, with a toy soldier's defined muscle and the status of a blue-chip back. "They'd go at it all the time, challenging each other," says mother Shonda. "They'd run the 40."

Mark Sr. was a gifted player with pronged hands who secured every catch and also earned bragging rights with an alltime highlight: He skirted five Buffalo Bills on a third-down play that kept alive a New York Giants TD drive in Super Bowl XXV.

His son grew up seeing his father play and, at times, hearing just how high expectations can be. "We'd be in a stadium and the fans would say things, and not always nice things," says Shonda. "I think growing up with that helped Mark mature."

Mark Jr. is all at once trying to separate himself from his father the pro while maintaining a tether to his dad's love. Whatever emotional and financial burdens have been freighted on the family due to Big Mark's choices—he has been in legal trouble since 2001, when he was caught with counterfeit cash, and he ended up in Queens after he failed to report to a federal prison in Ashland, Ky., on Dec. 5, 2008, after being sentenced to 92 months on bank-fraud and money-laundering charges—those issues remain within the family circle. The Ingrams do not indulge in the Oprah-style public catharses that are so common in a tell-all society. This is how they cope: by trying to live normally.

In Tuscaloosa, you can still catch the campus celebrity around midnight at a Wendy's, where he reveals a quirk of taste: He always dips his fries in a chocolate Frosty. You can still catch him cruising around town with a bag of sunflower seeds at hand and Lil' Wayne on the stereo. "That's about all he needs to be happy," says Tide safety Robby Green, Ingram's closest friend on the team.

Little Mark is smiling at the end of a YouTube clip from 2007—a piece about his father, titled *Mark Ingram: In His Own Words*. During the six-minute video the elder Ingram says, "When you come into a situation where you think you have a way of being slick, beating the system, it'll always come back to bite you in the butt." At the end the camera pans to the backdrop. Little Mark is working out on the track. He walks over to his father, who rubs his son's head and says, "That's my dude. He's going to be all right."

He is doing just fine—as his father can see.

FIRST TIMER Remarkably, no Alabama player had finished higher than third in the Heisman voting before Ingram was voted the 2009 award.

UNIT UNITY Defensive back Javier Arenas (28) and offensive lineman Mike Johnson (78) had reason to celebrate. | *Photograph by* RICHARD MACKSON

ORANGE CRUSHED Lineman Lorenzo Washington (97) and linebacker Rolando McClain (25) put the hurt on running back Tre' Newton. | *Photograph by* ROBERT BECK

RED MEET Here are four reasons why Texas was held to 81 rushing yards: Lorenzo Washington (left), Terrence Cody (62), Rolando McClain (25) and Mark Barron (4). | *Photograph by* BOB ROSATO

GAINING SEPARATION Mark Ingram took it in for the touchdown that put the Tide up by 10 in the fourth quarter. | *Photograph by* ROBERT BECK

POUND WISE McClain and Eryk Anders, two of 'Bama's defensive leaders, combined for a stop on Texas's Cody Johnson. | *Photograph by* JOHN BIEVER

THE TITLE GAME

BY ALBERT CHEN

Alabama had to survive some fourth-quarter drama to defeat Texas 37–21 and seize its first national championship in 17 years. Soon afterward players predicted that the wait for another would not be nearly as long. —excerpted from SI, JANUARY 13, 2010

A BALMY, POSTCARD-PERFECT SoCal afternoon had turned into a chilly night, and as the BCS national championship game between No. 1 Alabama and No. 2 Texas waned into its final minutes, the crimson-and-white-clad faithful who blanketed the west side of the Rose Bowl all wondered the same thing: How on earth could this be happening? Alabama had held a seemingly insurmountable 24–6 halftime lead. The Longhorns' star quarterback, Colt McCoy, had been knocked out on his team's fifth snap of the game. The ironclad Alabama defense had stifled a Texas offense thrown into chaos by a freshman backup quarterback nearly all night. And yet here were the Longhorns, with the ball and 3:14 left on the clock, trailing by only a field goal. The crowd of 94,906 was on its feet. Watching the game through sunglasses from the Texas sideline was Vince Young, the former Longhorns quarterback who had marched his team down this same field in the final minutes of the 2005 championship to lead Texas to a stunning upset of USC. Was another Texas miracle in the making?

The 'Bama defense, so dominant in the first half but listless for much of the game's second act, quickly answered that question. On first down from his own 17-yard line, Texas backup quarterback Garrett Gilbert, a true freshman who had completed just 15 passes as a Longhorn before this evening, dropped back to throw and was throttled by Alabama linebacker Eryk Anders, who had dashed untouched around the right defensive end on a blind-side blitz. Gilbert never stood a chance; the ball popped loose and rolled to the three-yard line, where it was smothered by Crimson Tide linebacker Courtney Upshaw.

In a bone-crunching contest that would have made even Bear Bryant crack a smile, this was the signature moment— "the difference-maker in the game," Alabama coach Nick Saban would later say. After running back Mark Ingram rumbled in for the touchdown three plays later, the Tide

faithful could exhale: Another national championship was on its way to Tuscaloosa.

Alabama's 37–21 win over Texas in Pasadena on Jan. 7 wasn't a masterpiece, unlike the Tide's dismantling of Florida in the SEC championship game. It wasn't pretty, not with quarterback Greg McElroy passing for just 58 yards on 11 attempts and the offense sputtering for most of the night (263 total yards to Texas's 276 and just two third-down conversions). But for a once-proud program that since its last championship season in 1992 had endured NCAA violations, ill-fated coaching hires and long stretches of mediocrity, it certainly would do. Under a rainstorm of confetti, as "Rammer Jammer" echoed across the old stadium in the shadows of the San Gabriel Mountains, Ingram, the Heisman Trophy winner and the game's offensive MVP, flashed a smile and made a proclamation that rang across the college football world as a new decade—a new era, perhaps—began. "Alabama's back," he said.

In the days leading up to the title game there was a lot of talk in Pasadena about the past—talk of Bear Bryant and Darrell Royal, talk of this Crimson Tide team bringing the glory back to a storied program—but with Alabama's convincing win there was also a sense that this was perhaps the beginning of a new dynasty in college football. In the locker room after the game almost every one of the team's underclassmen spoke about how they planned to be on the same stage a year from now. "We have something special going on here," said McElroy, who after the game revealed that he had cracked two ribs in the SEC championship game and couldn't throw a football for nearly two weeks. "Hopefully this is something we can build on, and hopefully we're back in this position a year from now. But this is a big start, and a big moment for Alabama."

The night was perhaps biggest for the stoic Saban, who in his third season at Alabama made history by becoming the first coach since the AP poll began in 1936 to win a national championship at two different schools. (He took LSU to the title in 2003.) Statues of Alabama's quartet of coaching greats—Bryant, Gene Stallings, Frank Thomas and Wallace Wade—line an area outside Bryant–Denny Stadium in Tuscaloosa. After the game the silver-haired Mal Moore, Alabama's longtime athletic director, stood outside the Crimson Tide locker room and talked about how he was already planning to lobby university president Robert Witt to commission a fifth statue: one of Saban, Alabama's newest hero. ◇

HIT, PARADE Anders's sack and forced fumble shut down Texas's comeback and assured that Alabama fans would be celebrating.

RECOVERY MISSION After Anders's hit jarred the ball loose from Gilbert with 3:08 left in the game and Texas down by three, Courtney Upshaw was there to pounce on the fumble. | *Photograph by* ROBERT BECK

BATH TIME Even after his players gave him a celebratory Gatorade dump, Saban continued to coach. | *Photograph by* PETER READ MILLER

GLOVE LOVE With Alabama's 13th championship close at hand, Ingram hailed with the houndstooth. | *Photograph by* STEPHEN DUNN/GETTY IMAGES

Acknowledgments

THESE PAGES are a tribute to the work of many brilliant writers and photographers who have covered Alabama football for SPORTS ILLUSTRATED over the decades. This book also would not have been possible without invaluable contributions from members of the SI staff, including Neil Cohen, Stefanie Kaufman, Lars Anderson, Claire Bourgeois, Cristina Scalet, Rich Donnelly, Denis Johnston, Lily Fine, Steve Fine, Chris Hercik, Gabe Miller, Nancy Ramsey, Karen Carpenter, Geoffrey Michaud, Dan Larkin, Bobby Thompson, Jeff Weig and Kari Stein. Special thanks to the Paul W. Bryant Museum, and to SI Group Editor Terry McDonell for his guidance, support and sharp eye.

ADDITIONAL PHOTO CREDITS
Table of contents (Top to bottom from left):
Neil Leifer, Bob Rosato, Walter Iooss Jr.,
Robert Beck, Walter Iooss Jr., Bob Rosato,
Neil Leifer, David Bergman, Walter Iooss Jr.
Book jacket end papers (front and back): Bill Frakes

TIME INC. HOME ENTERTAINMENT
Richard Fraiman, *Publisher;* Steven Sandonato,
General Manager; Carol Pittard, *Executive Director,
Marketing Services;* Tom Mifsud, *Director, Retail &
Special Sales;* Peter Harper, *Director, New Product
Development;* Laura Adam, *Assistant Director,
Bookazine Marketing;* Joy Butts, *Assistant Publishing
Director, Brand Marketing;* Helen Wan, *Associate
Counsel;* Anne-Michelle Gallero, *Design & Prepress
Manager;* Susan Chodakiewicz, *Book Production
Manager;* Allison Parker, *Associate Brand Manager*

BEARING DOWN Fans celebrated their icon at the 1980 Sugar Bowl.

UNIVERSITY OF ALABAMA
Paul "Bear" Bryant - Head Coach
1958 - 1982
NATIONAL COACH OF THE YEAR:
1961 · 1971 · 1973
·ALABAMA·
6-TIME NATIONAL CHAMP:
1961. 1964. 1965.
1973. 1978. 1979
Alabama
13 S.E.C. CROWNS
UNDER COACH BRYANT
BAMA·21